HARCOURT

· T R O P H I E S ·

A HARCOURT READING/LANGUAGE ARTS PROGRAM

ON YOUR MARK

SENIOR AUTHORS
Isabel L. Beck ◆ Roger C. Farr ◆ Dorothy S. Strickland

AUTHORS
Alma Flor Ada ◆ Marcia Brechtel ◆ Margaret McKeown
Nancy Roser ◆ Hallie Kay Yopp

SENIOR CONSULTANT
Asa G. Hilliard III

CONSULTANTS
F. Isabel Campoy ◆ David A. Monti

Harcourt

Orlando   Boston   Dallas   Chicago   San Diego

Visit *The Learning Site!*

www.harcourtschool.com

Acknowledgments appear in the back of this book.

Printed in the United States of America

ISBN 0-15-339786-1

7 8 9 10   048   10 09 08 07 06 05

Dear Reader,

Are you ready? You are about to travel on an exciting path. You may be surprised at how much you learn on the way.

In **On Your Mark,** the stories, poems, and articles will take you to many exciting places. Some places are in the past, some are in outer space, and some are at the center of the earth! You will meet many unusual characters and read about interesting facts. Some stories might even make you laugh out loud.

As you read this book, you will learn to be a better reader. You will learn about many new and interesting topics. Take the time to enjoy everything you learn along this reading journey.

On your mark, get set, read!

Sincerely,

The Authors

The Authors

TELL ME A STORY

CONTENTS

Reading
Across
Texts

Reading
Across
Texts

5

Good Neighbors

CONTENTS

Celebrate Our World

CONTENTS

Reading **Across** Texts

9

Using Reading Strategies

A strategy is a plan for doing something well.

You probably already use some strategies as you read. For example, you may **look at the title and pictures before you begin reading** a story. You may **think about what you want to find out while reading.** Using strategies like these can help you become a better reader.

Look at the list of strategies on page 11. You will learn about and use these strategies as you read the selections in this book. As you read, look back at the list to remind yourself of the **strategies good readers use.**

- Use Decoding/ Phonics

- Make and Confirm Predictions

- Create Mental Images

- Self-Question

- Summarize

- Read Ahead

- Reread to Clarify

- Use Context to Confirm Meaning

- Use Text Structure and Format

- Adjust Reading Rate

Here are some ways to check your own comprehension:

✔ Make a copy of this list on a piece of construction paper shaped like a bookmark.

✔ Have it handy as you read.

✔ After reading, talk with a classmate about which strategies you used and why.

TELL ME A STORY

CONTENTS

▲ Papa Tells Chita a Story

Vocabulary Power

soldier

colonel

weary

brambles

urgent

stumbling

outstretched

In "Papa Tells Chita a Story," a father tells his daughter a story. The story is about something that happened to him while serving in the army. Many brave men and women have served in the armies of their countries.

A soldier who serves in the army must raise his hand to salute an officer. The officer who stands facing the soldiers is a **colonel**. That is his rank, or position, in the army. You can tell a colonel by the silver eagle on his shoulder.

These soldiers are **weary**, very tired. They have marched through wet land and thick, prickly plants called **brambles**. Wading through water may slow them down, but they keep going because their mission is **urgent** and they need to act quickly.

Often there are times when soldiers must help one another. If one soldier is **stumbling** and about to fall, he can be sure there will be someone nearby with **outstretched** arms to catch him.

**Vocabulary–Writing
CONNECTION**

How should people behave in an **urgent** situation? List three things they should do.

15

PAPA

Notable
Social Studies
Trade Book

Historical Fiction

Historical fiction is a story that is set in the past and portrays people, places, and events that did happen or could have happened.

In this selection, look for

- the setting to be in a real time and place of the past.

- some made-up events and details.

16

Tells CHITA a STORY

by Elizabeth Fitzgerald Howard

illustrated by Floyd Cooper

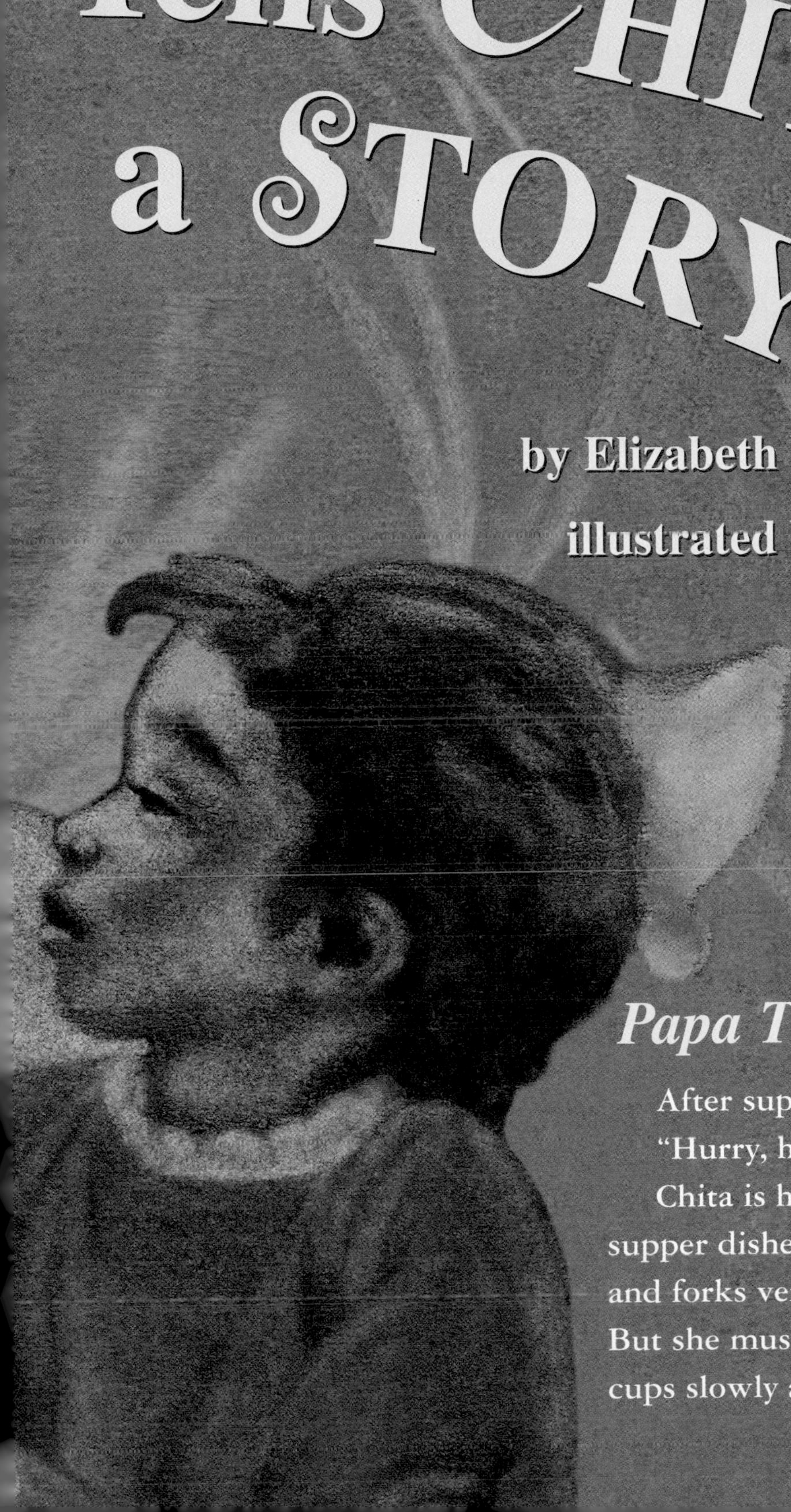

@

Papa Time, Chita Time

After supper is Papa time for Chita. "Hurry, hurry, Mama," says Chita. Chita is helping Mama with the supper dishes. She can dry the spoons and forks very quickly, *whisk, whisk*. But she must dry the china plates and cups slowly and very carefully.

17

Papa is sitting in his big chair by the fireplace. He has had a busy day helping sick patients. Some came to his office at home, just next to the living room. Some he went out to see in their own houses. Papa rode to his house calls in the big buggy pulled along by Henry the horse.

But now Papa is resting and reading and waiting for Chita. After supper is Chita time for Papa.

A Story, a Story

"Papa, I'm ready!" Chita pulls her own small chair close to Papa's big one.

"A story, a story. What story shall we have tonight?" Papa asks.

"Papa, Papa," pleads Chita, "tell about how you were the bravest soldier and carried the message and won the war!"

Papa smiles. "All right, my muchachita {mⁱoo • chä • chē´ tä}, I will tell you about those exciting days. And you can help me tell this story!"

Brave Papa

"Once, when I was a young man, I decided to become a doctor. I had to earn some money to go to medical school, so I joined the army and went off to fight in the Spanish War.

"I had just arrived in Cuba when the colonel called us all together.

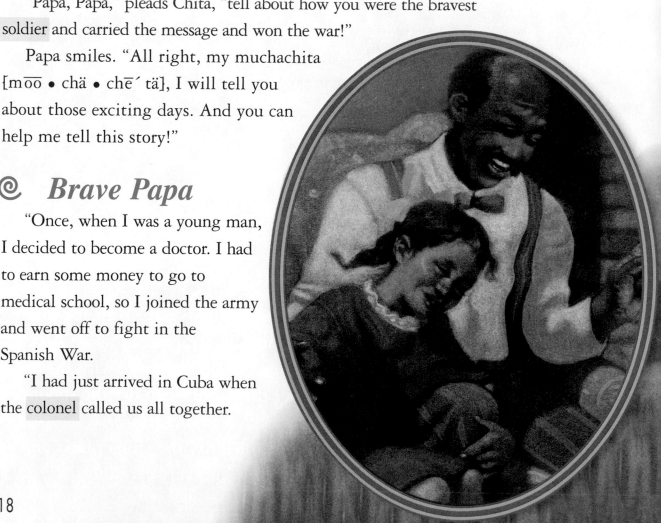

"'Men,' he said, 'we don't have enough soldiers to capture this hill. And we must have more supplies. I need someone very brave to carry a secret message to our troops across the island. It is a long and dangerous trip. There are snakes and swamps . . .'"

"And alligators, Papa," whispers Chita with a shivery giggle.

"That's right, Chita, and a high hill covered with brambles and prickles. Then the colonel asked, 'Who will go? Who is my bravest soldier?'"

"And it was you, Papa! You said, 'I will go!'" shouts Chita.

"Well . . . I wanted to be brave," says Papa. "So I said, 'I will do it, sir.' The colonel gave me an oilskin pouch with a letter inside. And a canteen full of water. And a map. And Majestic, a dark sleek horse with a waving white tail.

"I left immediately, riding Majestic. It was fiercely hot in the tropical sun. We rode through wide fields of tall tall grass. Suddenly Majestic stopped. Something was slithering and sneaking in the tall tall grass. *Sswushush . . . sswushush . . .* What could it be?"

"It was the big big BIG snake, Papa!"

"You're right, Chita! The snake was brown and round and as long as this living room. It raised up its head, squinted its beady eyes, and squinched toward us. But Majestic reared his front legs and zigzagged through the field, while I waved my sword and shouted strong words. We confused that snake, and it snake-snaked away in another direction."

"Hurray for Majestic! Hurray for Papa!" cries Chita. "And you kept on riding!"

"Well, I kept on riding, riding, riding . . . and the sun got hotter, hotter, hotter. And after a while we came to a great gray-green, greasy and slimy . . ."

"Swamp, Papa! It was the swamp!"

"Ugh! Chita! Ugh! I had to get through the swamp to reach the other side of the island. But Majestic would not move forward. I tried to persuade him. But he just stood there, still as a stone. I was disgusted. So I climbed down and told him, 'Good-bye. Go home, horse,' and he turned and headed back toward the colonel's camp. Then I stepped into the wet ooze. I held the colonel's oilskin pouch tight. Ooh, it was dreadful. I got in deeper and deeper. And just as I was about halfway across . . . "

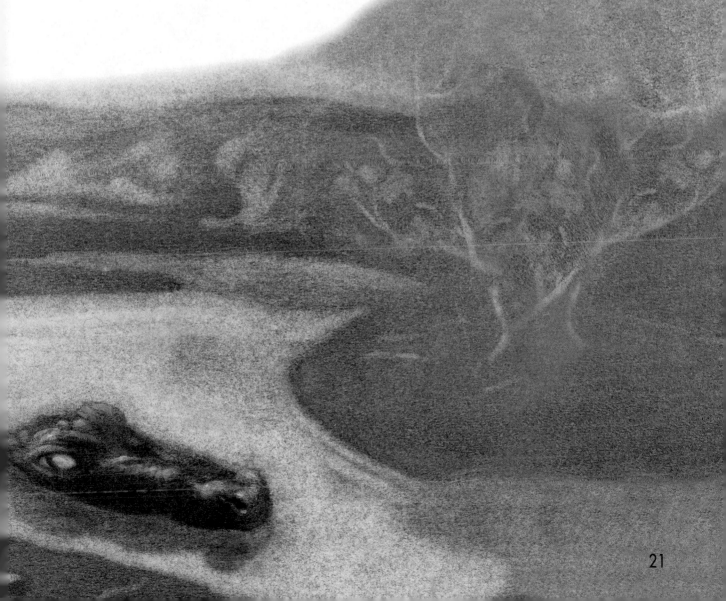

"The alligator, Papa!"

"Yes, indeedy, Chita! That alligator eyed me and came swimming steadily toward me. He yawned open his wide mouth, and I could count his sharp teeth. What could I do? I stuck the oilskin pouch deep into my shirt and hoped the message would be safe. Then I took a big breath, ducked under, and started swimming. Hard work in the mucky slime, with that alligator thrashing about above me! *Gluoosh . . .glush . . .gluoosh!*"

"And you swam right under the alligator, Papa, didn't you?" giggles Chita.

"Just swam right under him! Ha! I tricked the old rascal! He couldn't catch me! At last I climbed out onto dry land. I had lost my sword, and lost my canteen . . . but . . ."

"But the oilskin pouch was safe, Papa!"

"Yes, Chita. And, ooch, I was so sticky and muddy . . . but luckily I came to a waterfall. I stood under the cool cool tumbling water and washed off all the slimy ooze. But by now it was getting dark."

"And you were a teeny teeny bit scared, Papa!"

"A teeny teeny bit, Chita! And wet. And tired. But in front of me was a high hill."

"Very very high," says Chita. "And covered with brambles and prickles!"

"And I wondered if I could climb through all that thick underbrush. But I had to do it. I climbed and I crawled. And I crawled and I climbed. The brambles and prickles scratched my arms and legs. By the light of the moon I kept crawling and climbing, and at last—about midnight—I got to the top!"

"And you saw the big bird's nest, Papa!"

"Oh yes, Chita. In the moonlight I saw what looked like a big bird's nest! And it was empty! I was so weary and worn that I took a chance. I climbed in, curled up, and fell asleep."

"And then you heard the very very scary noise, Papa!" Chita whispers.

"You're right, Chita! I woke up to a loud screeching sound. *Skreeeeeech!* Help! I nearly jumped out of my skin! A giant eagle was scolding because somebody was in her nest!"

"Papa, *you* were in her nest!"

"She flew toward me with her claws outstretched. *Skreech! Skreeeeech!* I was terrified. I scrambled out and started stumbling my way down the other side of the hill. It was rough and tough, and I was scratched and sore. . . . After a long time, when I was almost at the bottom . . ."

"It was getting light! And you could smell something, Papa!" cheers Chita.

"What was it, Chita?"

"Papa, you could smell the smoke from a campfire!"

"And just over there I could see tents . . . and . . . yes, an American flag!"

"It was the soldiers, the American soldiers!" shouts Chita.

"You're right, Chita!" says Papa. "I went up to the officer in charge. 'Sir,' I said, 'I am Private McCard. I have brought an urgent message from the colonel.' And I handed him the oilskin pouch. 'Thank you,' said the officer. He took out the letter and read the message. Then he looked at me. 'McCard, you are extraordinarily brave. I will send more soldiers to the colonel immediately.'"

"And he sent more soldiers. And you went with them. And everybody was brave. But I think you were the bravest, Papa!"

☉ *What Is True?*

Chita jumps up and hugs Papa. Then she takes an old hat down from a peg on the wall and puts it on her head. And she takes a worn-looking belt from the bookcase and buckles it around her waist. "Here is your hat from the war, Papa! And here is your belt." And then, proudly, she pulls open a small drawer in Papa's big desk.

"And here is your beautiful medal!" Chita beams. She holds up a bronze medal with a red, white, and blue ribbon tied through it and hands it to Papa.

"You're right, Chita," Papa replies with a smile and a faraway look in his eyes. He turns the medal around and around in his hands.

"Papa, is that a true story?" Chita asks. Chita always likes to ask Papa if something is true.

"Well, my little muchachita," says Papa. "Some is true, and some is not true. But this is my true soldier's hat, and this is my true soldier's belt. And this is my true medal for being a brave soldier in the Spanish War. All that is true." Papa tweaks Chita's nose. "But do you know what else is true?"

"What, Papa!"

"It's true that you are a very good girl, and that Mama is waiting for you! Because it's time to go to bed!"

"Papa, you're a funny man," Chita says as she squeezes him a goodnight hug.

"Good night, Papa!"

"Good night, Chita!"

Think and Respond

1 Why does Chita love to hear Papa tell this story?

2 Why does Papa sometimes ask Chita what comes next?

3 Why did Papa run away when he saw the eagle with her claws **outstretched**?

4 Do you think the events happened exactly the way Papa tells about them? Why or why not?

5 How did using a reading strategy help you with this story? Give an example.

Elizabeth Fitzgerald Howard

Elizabeth Fitzgerald Howard thinks back to her own childhood in Maryland for her stories. She loves to write about her family members in her books. In *Papa Tells Chita a Story*, you meet her father's cousin Chita. Elizabeth Howard wants her readers to discover both how they are like other children and how they are different and special.

Floyd Cooper

Floyd Cooper says a strong imagination helps him in his work. When he first reads a story, he likes to sit back and think about it for awhile. He imagines everything in it—the place, the weather, the sights, the smells, and the sounds.

Floyd learned to draw people in the seventh grade when a teacher gave him a book on the human body. Today, he sometimes uses photographs to help him draw people. Other times, he uses his friends as models. In addition to illustrating children's books, he has painted portraits of people and made pictures for greeting cards.

Chita and her Papa, Harry S. McCard.

Elizabeth
Fitzgerald
Howard

Floyd Cooper

Making Connections

Compare Texts

1. Why does Papa make up details and events when he tells Chita about being a soldier?

2. Why is the story divided into sections with subheadings, such as "A Story, A Story"?

3. How is *telling* a story, as Papa does, different from reading a story from a book?

4. Think of a story someone in your family has told you about his or her own life. How was that story like Papa's story? How was it different?

5. Do you think Chita will ask Papa to tell this same story again? Why or why not?

Write a Caption

Story illustrations show events that the story tells about. Think about your favorite illustration for "Papa Tells Chita a Story." Write to explain in your own words what is happening in the illustration. Use a graphic organizer like this one to plan what you will write.

Writing CONNECTION

Illustration, page _____		
Character	Setting	Event

Role-Play a Hero

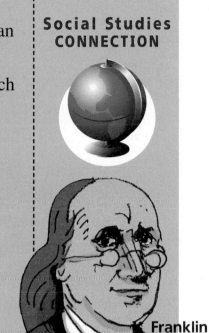

Papa was a brave soldier in the Spanish-American War. Other kinds of heroes have helped to make the United States a great and free nation. Research an American hero. After you have gathered information about your hero, prepare a role-play of that person. Tell about what you did for our country. Practice and present your role-play.

King

Franklin

Create a Bulletin Board Display

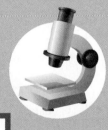

Alligators are close relatives of crocodiles, but they are different animals. Do some research to find out about differences between alligators and crocodiles. Create a bulletin board display about these reptiles. You might include a chart or labeled drawing showing the differences between the two. You could also show where each animal is found.

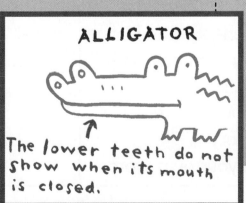

ALLIGATOR

The lower teeth do not show when its mouth is closed.

Summarize

Summarizing is telling the important ideas in a story in your own words. Read this summary of "Papa Tells Chita a Story."

> Papa tells Chita a story about the time he carried a special message when he was a soldier. He tells about meeting a big snake, swimming under an alligator, and sleeping in an eagle's nest. When Chita asks if the story is true, Papa tells her that some of it is true and some is not.

What Should a Good Summary Do?

IT SHOULD	IT SHOULD NOT
• tell about the most important ideas or the main things that happened in the story • follow the same order as the story • be much shorter than the story • be in your own words	• tell about things that are not important to the story • tell about things that are not in the story • give your own ideas or opinions

Test Prep
Summarize

▶ **Read the story.**

Grandmother's Story

When Grandmother was a little girl, there was a great flood. Marcus never gets tired of hearing her tell about it. "The water rose higher and higher," Grandmother says. "The water in the street was up to my ankles, then up to my knees, and it kept rising." She tells how people used rowboats and canoes to get around town. Marcus's favorite part of her story and the part he doesn't quite believe is about the big pig that swam right down the middle of Main Street.

Now answer numbers 1 and 2.
Base your answers on the story.

1. **Which sentence would not be included in a good summary?**

   A Grandmother tells about a pig that swims.

   B Marcus loves to hear the story.

   C I don't believe that pigs can really swim.

   D Grandmother tells Marcus about a flood.

2. **Write a summary of the story in one or two sentences.**

Tip

Remember that a good summary does not give your own ideas or opinions.

Tip

Tell the most important ideas from the story in your own words.

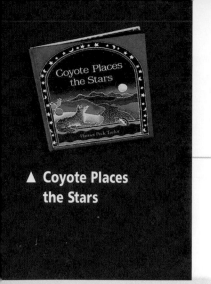

▲ Coyote Places
the Stars

Vocabulary Power

Can animals talk? Can animals have a feast? Sometimes things happen in stories that can't happen in real life. Read to find out about these animals and their talents.

swiftly

skillful

canyon

gazing

pride

feast

arranged

I'm a fast runner. Don't you wish you could run as **swiftly** as I do?

I don't worry about running fast. I'm a **skillful** climber. I have a talent for climbing trees.

I don't have to run or climb. I can fly to the top of the tallest tree, or swoop quickly through a deep **canyon**.

I am **gazing** at all of you. I can see that you have a lot of **pride** in the things you can do. Each of you is happy that you can do something well. I would like to invite you to a **feast**. It will be a special celebration with lots of good food.

Using their special talents, the animals **arranged** the feast. They carefully set out berries and nuts in celebration of each of their talents.

Vocabulary-Writing CONNECTION

Write a short paragraph that describes an animal that moves **swiftly**. Include words that tell how the animal looks as it moves.

Coyote Places
the Stars

Harriet Peck Taylor

Coyote

Coyote

retold and illustrated by
Harriet Peck Taylor

Many moons and many moons ago lived in a canyon by a swift-runr spent his days roaming the land, chasi and sniffing wildflowers. He lay awake gazing at the starry heavens.

One summer night, as he was relaxi grass with his friend Bear, Coyote had a think I will climb to the heavens and di secrets!"

Bear scratched his big head and aske you do that?"

"I can get up there with no trouble at said.

Now, Coyote was very skillful with a b He gathered a very large pile of arrows a shoot them at the sky. The first arrow wh the air and landed on the moon. Coyote second arrow, which caught in the notch *Whi-rr* went one arrow. *Whizz* went the n and on until this long line of arrows mac

Coyote then began to climb. He climb days and nights until he finally reached He slept all that day, as he was very tired

Places the Stars

39

That night Coyote had another clever idea. He wondered if he could move the stars around by shooting at them with his remaining arrows. His first arrow hit a star and moved it across the sky. He found he could place the stars wherever he wanted.

Coyote wagged his bushy tail and yelped for joy. He was going to make pictures in the sky for all the world to see.

First he decided to make a coyote, so he shot one arrow after another until the stars were arranged in the shape of a coyote. Next he thought of his friend Bear, and placed the stars in the form of a bear.

Coyote worked all night creating likenesses of all his
friends—Mountain Lion, Horse, Goat, Fish, Owl, and Eagle.
With the stars he had left over, he made a Big Road across
the sky. When he was finished, he began to descend his
ladder back to earth.

That night, when the bright moon rose in the
east, Coyote saw his handiwork and began to howl.
Oweowowooooah was carried on the wind through the
shadows of the canyon. Birds and animals awoke suddenly
and listened to the mysterious sound. It seemed to be
calling to them. From canyons and mesas, hills and plains
they came, following the sound.

Bears bounded out of their dens. Squirrels scampered and rabbits hippity-hopped over the hills. Bobcats crept and bristly porcupines waddled along the trail.

Graceful deer moved swiftly, while lizards slowly crawled across the desert.

Silvery fish splashed their way upstream. The mighty mountain lion and herds of buffalo joined the journey.

The great eagle soared over moonlit mountains. On and on went the parade of animals, following Coyote's magical voice.

Finally Coyote appeared, high on a rock. The animals formed a huge circle and all became quiet. Coyote's eyes blazed with pride as he said, "Animals and birds and all who are gathered here: Please look at the sky. You will see the stars are arranged in the shapes of animals. I made a ladder to the moon, and from there I shot my arrows to create the pictures you see."

As the animals looked up, a great chorus of whoofing and whiffing, screeching and squawking filled the air.

"I made a coyote and my friend Bear. You will see the mysterious Owl, the great Eagle, the Goat, Horse, Fish, and the mighty Mountain Lion. This is my handiwork, and I hope that all who see it will remember Coyote and all the animals of the canyon."

The animals gave a great feast for Coyote, and they sang and danced through the night. The animals decreed that Coyote was the most clever and crafty of all the animals.

Coyote was so grateful that he declared, "I will always be your friend and the friend of your children's children."

Now, to this day, if you listen closely in the still of the night as the moon is rising, you may even hear the magical howl of Coyote. He is calling you to go to your window, to gaze at the star pictures, and to dream.

Think and Respond

1 How does Coyote place the stars? Why does he do it?

2 Why do the animals give a great **feast** for coyote?

3 How does this story explain why Coyote howls?

4 What pictures would you have made if you had **arranged** the stars?

5 How did using a reading strategy help you read this selection?

Meet the Author and Illustrator

Harriet Peck Taylor

Coyote Places the Stars was my first book. It is based on several Native American legends that explain the starry sky. During the time I was writing this book, I met a real coyote. Every day he would follow me on my daily hike. Sometimes the coyote would howl to me. One day I didn't see him, so I tried to make a wolflike howl. To my surprise, he howled back and came out where I could see him. Seeing that coyote helped me paint the pictures for my book.

These illustrations are done with a type of painting called batik. Batik is an ancient artform that uses dyes and hot wax on cotton fabric.

 Visit *The Learning Site!*
www.harcourtschool.com

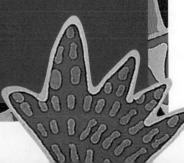

Starry, Starry Night

★by James Muirden★

Have you ever tried to count the stars? On dark nights you can see hundreds. There are lots more you can't see, though, because they are so faint they can be found only by using a telescope.

Astronomers are people who study the stars. They think there may be a hundred million million million stars altogether. That's 100,000,000,000,000,000,000!

Galileo was the first person to use the telescope to look at stars.

Secrets of
the Stars

Stars look tiny from Earth.
But if you could visit one,
this is the sort of thing
you'd find . . .

a vast, scorching-hot ball of
glowing gas—much like our
sun, because the sun is
actually our nearest star!

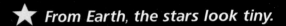

 From Earth, the stars look tiny.

If you could take a closer look,
you might see this.

No Sunday Drive

The sun may be a close neighbor, but it's still 93 million miles away from us. It would take about 150 years to travel that far in a car!

We would all be fried if the sun were any nearer, though, because it gives off as much heat as 1,000 million million million million space heaters all switched on at once. Temperatures at the center of the sun are about 27 million °F.

Star Light, Star Bright

The sun is dazzlingly bright, too. You should NEVER look directly at it. Its light is so strong it could harm your eyes, even on hazy days.

Even so, the sun is not particularly hot or bright compared with other stars. And although a million Earths could fit inside it, it isn't all that big either.

Some of those tiny twinkling lights you see on starry nights are gigantic. They are big enough for a million stars like our sun to fit inside them!

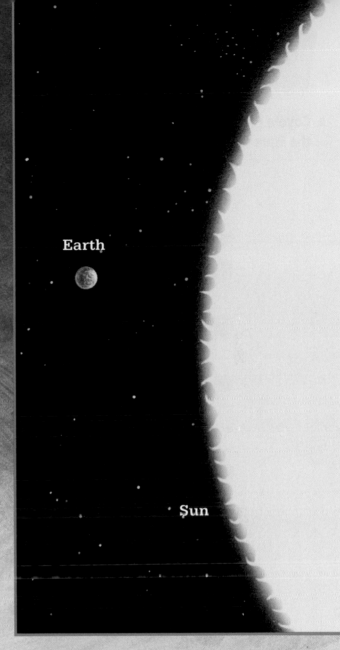

Earth

Sun

Think and Respond

What does the article tell us about our sun and other stars?

Making Connections

Compare Texts

1 What things in nature does this story explain?

2 Why do you think the illustrator uses two whole pages for the illustration on pages 46–47?

3 How are the selections "Coyote Places the Stars" and "Starry, Starry Night" alike? How are they different?

4 What is another story you have read that has talking animal characters? Which story would you choose to read aloud to a younger child? Tell why.

5 Has reading this story made you more interested in looking at the stars? Explain your answer.

Write a Set of Directions

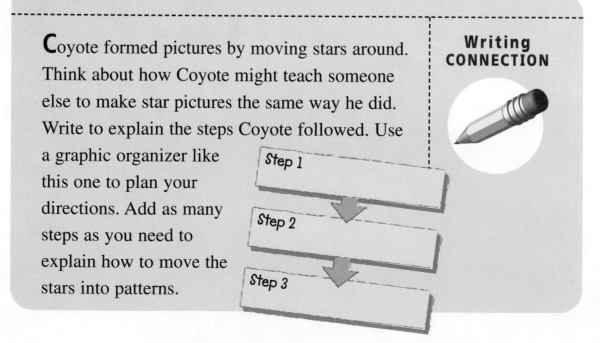

Coyote formed pictures by moving stars around. Think about how Coyote might teach someone else to make star pictures the same way he did. Write to explain the steps Coyote followed. Use a graphic organizer like this one to plan your directions. Add as many steps as you need to explain how to move the stars into patterns.

Writing CONNECTION

Step 1

Step 2

Step 3

56

Draw a Diagram

Stars that make up the constellations can be seen from Earth. How long does it take the light from the stars to reach Earth? How long does it take light to travel from an object on Earth so that you can see it? Use reference sources to find out. Compare the difference in time for different objects. Share your findings on a poster or diagram.

Science CONNECTION

Prepare an Oral Report

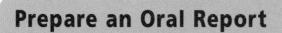

Harriet Peck Taylor uses an art form called batik for her illustrations in "Coyote Places the Stars." The design is made by putting hot wax on cloth. Colored dyc, or paint, will not stick to the waxed areas. Clay and paper are other art forms that artists use. Who are some well-known artists that use these and other art forms? Do research to answer this question. Prepare an oral report to share with your class.

Art CONNECTION

Compare and Contrast

When you **compare** things, you think about how they are **alike**. When you **contrast**, you think about how they are **different**.

You can compare and contrast the character Coyote with a real coyote by telling how they are alike and different.

Character Coyote   **Real Coyote**

ALIKE	DIFFERENT
Both live in the wild. Both howl at night.	Character can talk and shoot a bow; real coyotes cannot. Character is friends with all kinds of animals; real coyotes are not.

Visit _The Learning Site!_
www.harcourtschool.com

See _Skills_ and _Activities_

Test Prep
Compare and Contrast

Mole Plants a Garden

Once there was a mole who decided to plant a garden. Mole worked hard. He planted and weeded and watered. When the vegetables were ready to pick, Mole gave some to his friend, Mouse. They were so good that Mouse came every day to get more.

One day, Mole said, "Friend Mouse, I have lost my ring. Your eyesight is much sharper than mine. Will you help me find it?"

"Oh no, Mole, I can't help you," said Mouse. "I'm much too busy. Just give me some vegetables, and I'll be on my way."

▶ Use the story to answer questions 1 and 2.

1. The characters Mole and Mouse are alike because both—

   A are good at digging

   B wear gold rings

   C plant gardens

   D like vegetables

Tip

Read each choice. The correct choice is true for both characters, not just one of them.

2. How are the two characters different from each other?

   F Mouse is happy. Mole is sad.

   G Mole eats a lot. Mouse eats little.

   H Mole is generous. Mouse is selfish.

   J Mouse works hard. Mole is lazy.

Tip

Think about whether each choice is true and whether it describes a way the characters are different.

▲ Why Mosquitoes
Buzz in People's Ears

Vocabulary Power

council

duty

tidbit

nonsense

mischief

satisfied

Every neighborhood has problems from time to time. This article tells how some neighbors got together to talk about their problems.

Neighbors Talk About Problems

People living near Glenwood Park have been hearing that the city has plans to tear down houses in their neighborhood. Last night, people in the neighborhood held a **council**. The meeting was called to clear up the confusion people were feeling.

Mariana Sanchez was chosen to head the council. Her **duty** is to run the meetings. She invited the mayor to this meeting.

People at the meeting talked and talked. The mayor said that people should not believe every **tidbit** of gossip they hear. Soon the neighbors began to see that much of the gossip was **nonsense**. The ideas were foolish and could not be true. The mayor pointed out that gossip can lead to **mischief**. The people would not want behavior like that causing problems in their neighborhood.

Afterward, people said that they were **satisfied** with the meeting. Their questions were answered.

Vocabulary–Writing CONNECTION

Write two sentences that state a problem in the classroom, school, or community that a student **council** could address. Write a third sentence that suggests a solution to the problem.

Caldecott
Medal

West African Tale

A tale is a story that has been passed down through time.

In this selection, look for

- **animals that act like people.**
- **a character who learns a lesson.**

WHY BUZZ IN

A West African Tale

retold by Verna Aardema
pictures by Leo and Diane Dillon

MOSQUITOES
PEOPLE'S EARS

ONE MORNING a mosquito saw an iguana drinking at a waterhole. The mosquito said, "Iguana, you will never believe what I saw yesterday."

"Try me," said the iguana.

The mosquito said, "I saw a farmer digging yams that were almost as big as I am."

"What's a mosquito compared to a yam?" snapped the iguana grumpily. "I would rather be deaf than listen to such nonsense!" Then he stuck two sticks in his ears and went off, mek, mek, mek, mek, through the reeds.

The iguana was still grumbling to himself when he happened to pass by a python.

The big snake raised his head and said, "Good morning, Iguana."

The iguana did not answer but lumbered on, bobbing his head, badamin, badamin.

"Now, why won't he speak to me?" said the python to himself. "Iguana must be angry about something. I'm afraid he is plotting some mischief against me!" He began looking for somewhere to hide. The first likely place he found was a rabbit hole, and in it he went, wasawusu, wasawusu, wasawusu.

When the rabbit saw the big snake coming into her burrow, she was terrified. She scurried out through her back way and bounded, krik, krik, krik, across a clearing.

A crow saw the rabbit running for her life. He flew into the forest crying kaa, kaa, kaa! It was his duty to spread the alarm in case of danger.

A monkey heard the crow. He was sure that some dangerous beast was prowling near. He began screeching and leaping kili wili through the trees to help warn the other animals.

As the monkey was crashing through the treetops, he happened to land on a dead limb. It broke and fell on an owl's nest, killing one of the owlets.

Mother Owl was not at home. For though she usually hunted only in the night, this morning she was still out searching for one more tidbit to satisfy her hungry babies. When she returned to the nest, she found one of them dead. Her other children told her that the monkey had killed it. All that day and all that night, she sat in her tree—so sad, so sad, so sad!

Now it was Mother Owl who woke the sun each day so that the dawn could come. But this time, when she should have hooted for the sun, she did not do it.

The night grew longer and longer. The animals of the forest knew it was lasting much too long. They feared that the sun would never come back.

69

At last King Lion called a meeting of the animals. They came and sat down, pem, pem, pem, around a council fire. Mother Owl did not come, so the antelope was sent to fetch her.

When she arrived, King Lion asked, "Mother Owl, why have you not called the sun? The night has lasted long, long, long, and everyone is worried."

Mother Owl said, "Monkey killed one of my owlets. Because of that, I cannot bear to wake the sun."

The king said to the gathered animals:
"Did you hear?
It was the monkey
who killed the owlet —
and now Mother Owl won't wake the sun
so that the day can come."

Then King Lion called the monkey. He came before him nervously glancing from side to side, rim, rim, rim, rim.

"Monkey," said the king, "why did you kill one of Mother Owl's babies?"

"Oh, King," said the monkey, "it was the crow's fault. He was calling and calling to warn us of danger. And I went leaping through the trees to help. A limb broke under me, and it fell taaa on the owl's nest."

The king said to the council:
"So, it was the crow
who alarmed the monkey,
who killed the owlet —
and now Mother Owl won't wake the sun
so that the day can come."

Then the king called for the crow. That big
bird came flapping up. He said, "King Lion, it was
the rabbit's fault! I saw her running for her life in
the daytime. Wasn't that reason enough to spread
an alarm?"

The king nodded his head and said to the council:
"So, it was the rabbit
who startled the crow,
who alarmed the monkey,
who killed the owlet —
and now Mother Owl won't wake the sun
so that the day can come."

73

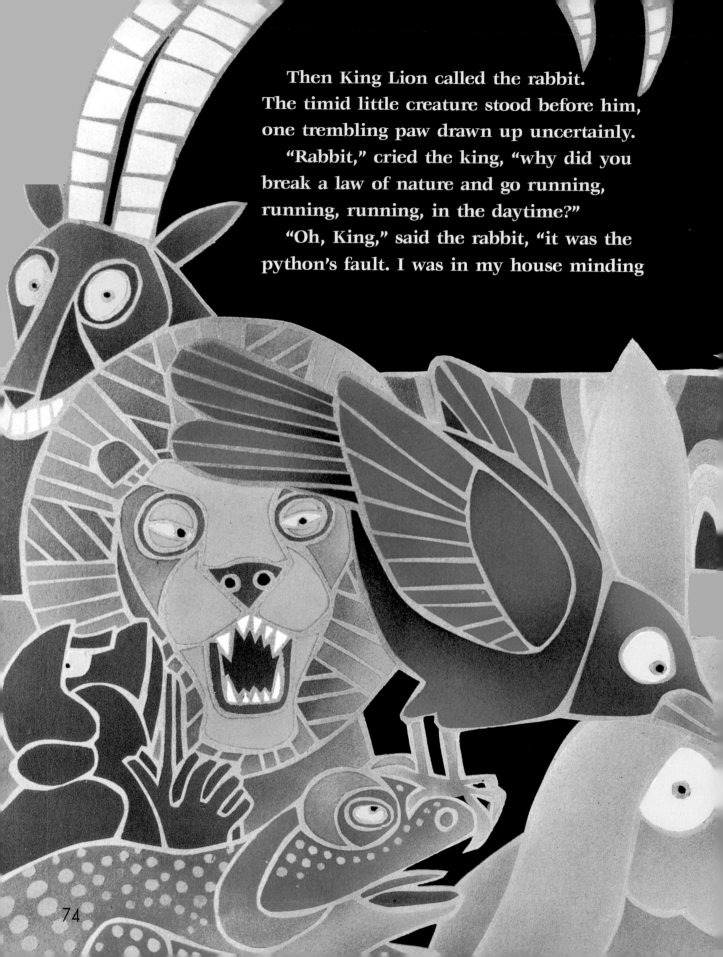

Then King Lion called the rabbit.
The timid little creature stood before him,
one trembling paw drawn up uncertainly.

"Rabbit," cried the king, "why did you
break a law of nature and go running,
running, running, in the daytime?"

"Oh, King," said the rabbit, "it was the
python's fault. I was in my house minding

my own business when that big snake came
in and chased me out."

The king said to the council:
"So, it was the python
who scared the rabbit,
who startled the crow,
who alarmed the monkey,
who killed the owlet —
and now Mother Owl won't wake the sun
so that the day can come."

King Lion called the python, who came slithering, wasawusu, wasawusu, past the other animals. "But, King," he cried, "it was the iguana's fault! He wouldn't speak to me. And I thought he was plotting some mischief against me. When I crawled into the rabbit's hole, I was only trying to hide."

The king said to the council:
"So, it was the iguana
who frightened the python,
who scared the rabbit,
who startled the crow,
who alarmed the monkey,
who killed the owlet—
and now Mother Owl won't wake the sun
so that the day can come."

Now the iguana was not at the meeting. For he had not heard the summons.

The antelope was sent to fetch him.

All the animals laughed when they saw the iguana coming, badamin, badamin, with the sticks still stuck in his ears!

King Lion pulled out the sticks, purup, purup.
Then he asked, "Iguana, what evil have you been
plotting against the python?"

"Nonc! None at all!" cried the iguana. "Python is
my friend!"

"Then why wouldn't you say good morning to
me?" demanded the snake.

"I didn't hear you, or even see you!" said the iguana. "Mosquito told me such a big lie, I couldn't bear to listen to it. So I put sticks in my ears."

"Nge, nge, nge," laughed the lion. "So that's why you had sticks in your ears!"

"Yes," said the iguana. "It was the mosquito's fault."

King Lion said to the council:
"So, it was the mosquito
who annoyed the iguana,
who frightened the python,
who scared the rabbit,

who startled the crow,
who alarmed the monkey,
who killed the owlet—
and now Mother Owl won't wake the sun
so that the day can come."

"Punish the mosquito! Punish the mosquito!"
cried all the animals.

When Mother Owl heard that, she was satisfied.
She turned her head toward the east and hooted:
"Hoo! Hooooo! Hooooooo!"

And the sun came up.

Meanwhile the mosquito had listened to it all from a nearby bush. She crept under a curly leaf, semm, and was never found and brought before the council.

But because of this the mosquito has a guilty conscience. To this day she goes about whining in people's ears: "Zeee! Is everyone still angry at me?"

When she does that, she gets an honest answer.

Think and Respond

1 How do the iguana's actions lead King Lion to call a **council** meeting?

2 What kind of tale is this? Why do you think it is still being told today?

3 Why does the mosquito have a guilty conscience?

4 Do you think the mosquito meant to do harm?

5 Give an example of a strategy you used while reading this story. How did it help you?

Meet the Illustrators

Leo and Diane Dillon

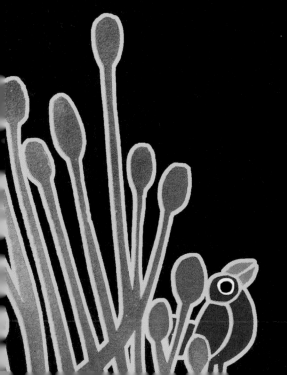

Leo and Diane Dillon have been working as a team for more than thirty years! They are married and work in New York City. But what did they do before they were a team?

When Leo Dillon was a boy, he drew pictures of everything he saw. Although his parents encouraged him to draw, they hoped he would become a lawyer or doctor. Unlike her husband, Diane Dillon didn't always want to be an artist. She thought about becoming a nurse. After taking a few art lessons, she decided to go to art school. That is where she met Leo Dillon.

The Dillons have worked together on book covers, magazines, posters, and children's books. When working on a picture together, they pass the drawing back and forth between them. They each draw one small section at a time. Their work has won them many awards, including two Caldecott Medals in a row!

Leo Dillon

Diane Dillon

Visit *The Learning Site!* www.harcourtschool.com

The Ant and the Grasshopper

RETOLD AND ILLUSTRATED
BY **AMY LOWRY POOLE**

A long time ago, in the old Summer Palace at the edge of the Emperor's courtyard, there lived a grasshopper and a family of ants.

The ants awoke every day before dawn and began their endless tasks of rebuilding their house of sand, which had been washed down by the evening rains, and searching for food, which they would store beneath the ground. They carried their loads grain by grain, one by one, back and forth, all day long.

The grasshopper liked to sleep late into the morning, rising as the sun stretched toward noon.

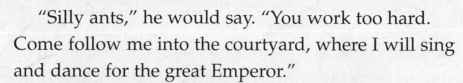

"Silly ants," he would say. "You work too hard. Come follow me into the courtyard, where I will sing and dance for the great Emperor."

The ants kept on working.

"Silly ants," the grasshopper would say. "See the new moon. Feel the summer breeze. Let us go together and watch the Empress and her ladies as they prepare for midsummer's eve."

But the ants ignored the grasshopper and kept on working.

Soon the days grew shorter and the wind brought cooler air from the north. The ants, mindful of the winter to come, worked even harder to secure their home against the impending cold and snow. They foraged for food and brought it back to their nest, saving it for those cold winter months.

"Silly ants," said the grasshopper. "Don't you ever rest? Today is the harvest festival. The Emperor will feast on mooncakes and sweet greens from the fields. I will play my music for him until the moon disappears into the smooth lake water. Come and dance with me."

"You would do well to do as we do," said one of the ants. "Winter is coming soon and food will be hard to find. Snow will cover your house and you will freeze without shelter."

But the grasshopper ignored the ant's advice and continued to play and dance until the small hours of the morning.

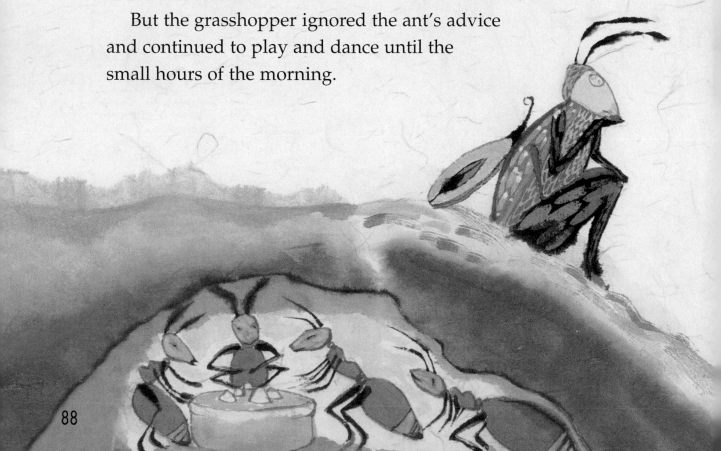

Winter arrived a week later and brought whirls of snow and ice. The Emperor and his court left the Summer Palace for their winter home in the great Forbidden City. The ants closed their door against the ice and snow, safe and warm, resting at last after their long days of preparation.

And the grasshopper huddled beneath the palace eaves and rubbed his hands together in a mournful chirp, wishing he had heeded the ant's advice.

Think and Respond

Why do the ants tell the grasshopper to work instead of playing all summer?

Making Connections

Compare Texts

1 Why do you think "Why Mosquitoes Buzz in People's Ears" is in a theme called Tell Me a Story?

2 Why does the author add words such as *mek, mek* to the story?

3 What is the difference between a folktale like "Why Mosquitoes Buzz in People's Ears" and a fable like "The Ant and the Grasshopper"?

4 Compare "Why Mosquitoes Buzz in People's Ears" with "Coyote Places the Stars." How are the two stories alike?

5 How might the animals in this story act differently in the future?

Write a Summons

King Lion sends a summons for the animals to come to the meeting. Think about what information a summons should contain and how a summons is different from a friendly invitation. Write a summons to inform a story character about the meeting. Use a graphic organizer like this one to plan your summons.

Writing CONNECTION

[Date]

Dear ___Antelope___,

_____

_____

_____

Sincerely,
King Lion

90

Make a Poster

Mother Owl's job is to wake the sun each day. This tale may have been passed down to explain the sun in the morning sky. Does the sun move across the sky? Do research to find out how the sun is related to the movement of Earth. Make a poster to explain the position of the sun in our sky at different times of the day or year.

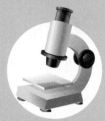

Science CONNECTION

Write a Song

The author of "Why Mosquitoes Buzz in People's Ears" repeats the words that stand for sounds in the forest or jungle. This gives a musical feeling to the story. Write a song that retells this folktale or another that you know. Follow these steps:

1. Decide on a tune for your song.
2. Look through the story to find nature sounds and words to use.
3. Write the words of your song to go with the tune you picked.
4. Practice your song.
5. Record your song, and share it with classmates.

Music CONNECTION

Summarize

You have learned that you summarize a story by telling the important ideas in your own words.

Reread page 65 of "Why Mosquitoes Buzz in People's Ears." Then read this summary of the events on page 65.

> **SUMMARY: The mosquito tells a silly story. The iguana puts sticks in his ears to keep from hearing it.**

Is this a good summary? Use the checklist to see.

> ### Summary Checklist
> ✔ **Does it tell only the most important ideas or events?**
> ✔ **Does it follow the same order as the story?**
> ✔ **Is it much shorter than the story?**
> ✔ **Is it told in different words?**
> ✔ **Does it tell only about things that are in the story?**

Test Prep
Summarize

▶ **Read the story.**

A Terrible Mess

It all began when the fish flipped its tail. Some water flew up and splashed the porcupine. When the porcupine shook itself to get dry, one of its quills flew out. The sharp quill hit the cottontail rabbit. In its fright, the rabbit jumped so high that it hit the branch of a big oak tree. The crow, who was sitting on the branch, got such a jolt that it flew away.

Now answer numbers 1 and 2. Base your answers on the story.

1. **What is the most important thing to tell about in a summary of this story?**

   A   that the rabbit was a cottontail

   B   that the crow was sitting in an oak tree

   C   that the crow flew away

   D   that one event led to another

2. **Write a summary of the story.**

Tip
Remember that a good summary tells only the most important ideas or events.

Tip
Tell the most important ideas or events from the story in your own words.

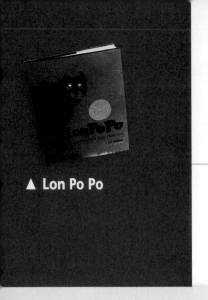

▲ Lon Po Po

tender

brittle

embraced

dusk

latch

cunning

delighted

Vocabulary Power

Do you know the story "Little Red Riding Hood"? If you do, you might remember that a wolf pretended to be Red Riding Hood's grandmother. There are many stories in which one character tries to trick another.

HENS: We had such a good dinner. We had **tender** grain, soft and easy to chew. We had **brittle** seeds that broke easily and snapped. We **embraced** each other in good-night hugs. Now it's **dusk**. It will soon be night, so it's time for us to go to bed.

FOX: Sisters! It's your sister Henrietta. I've come to visit. Why did you **latch** the door? Please unhook the latch and open the door.

(The eldest hen looks closely at the visitor.)

HENS: (whispering) This tricky fox thinks he's very **cunning**.
   He thinks we're a bunch of silly hens, but we're not.
   We're clever. We see what he's trying to do!

FOX: I'm **delighted** to be here! I'm filled with joy!

HENS: Go away, you bad fox, and don't come back!

**Vocabulary–Writing
CONNECTION**

How does the sky look at **dusk**? What colors might you see? Write a paragraph describing this time of day.

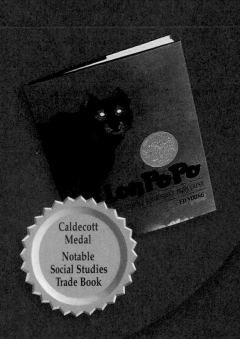

Genre

Folktale

**A folktale is a story
with no known author
that has been passed
down through time.**

In this selection, look for

- **familiar characters
  and plot in a different
  setting.**

- **an animal that behaves
  like a human.**

Lon Po Po

A RED·RIDING HOOD STORY FROM CHINA

translated and illustrated
by Ed Young

Once, long ago, there was a woman who lived alone in the country with her three children, Shang, Tao, and Paotze. On the day of their grandmother's birthday, the good mother set off to see her, leaving the three children at home.

Before she left, she said, "Be good while I am away, my heart-loving children; I will not return tonight. Remember to close the door tight at sunset and latch it well."

But an old wolf lived nearby and saw the good mother leave. At dusk, disguised as an old woman, he came up to the house of the children and knocked on the door twice: bang, bang.

Shang, who was the eldest, said through the latched door, "Who is it?"

"My little jewels," said the wolf, "this is your grand-mother, your Po Po."

"Po Po!" Shang said. "Our mother has gone to visit you!"

The wolf acted surprised. "To visit me? I have not met her along the way. She must have taken a different route."

"Po Po!" Shang said. "How is it that you come so late?"

The wolf answered, "The journey is long, my children, and the day is short."

Shang listened through the door. "Po Po," she said, "why is your voice so low?"

"Your grandmother has caught a cold, good children, and it is dark and windy out here. Quickly open up, and let your Po Po come in," the cunning wolf said.

Tao and Paotze could not wait. One unlatched the door and the other opened it. They shouted, "Po Po, Po Po, come in!"

At the moment he entered the door, the wolf blew out the candle.

"Po Po," Shang asked, "why did you blow out the candle? The room is now dark."

The wolf did not answer.

Tao and Paotze rushed to their Po Po and wished to be hugged. The old wolf held Tao. "Good child, you are so plump." He embraced Paotze. "Good child, you have grown to be so sweet."

Soon the old wolf pretended to be sleepy. He yawned. "All the chicks are in the coop," he said. "Po Po is sleepy too." When he climbed into the big bed, Paotze climbed in at one end with the wolf, and Shang and Tao climbed in at the other.

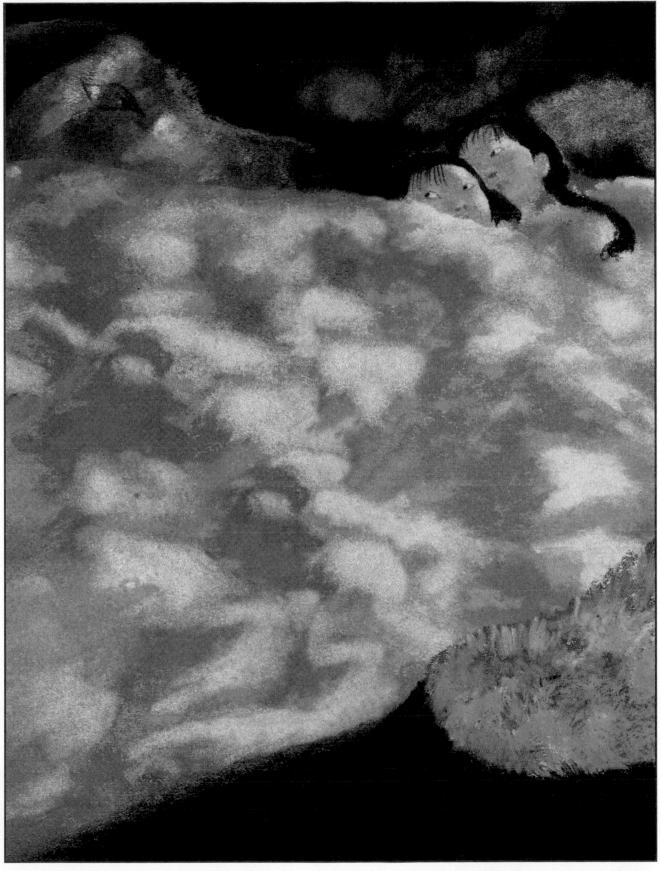

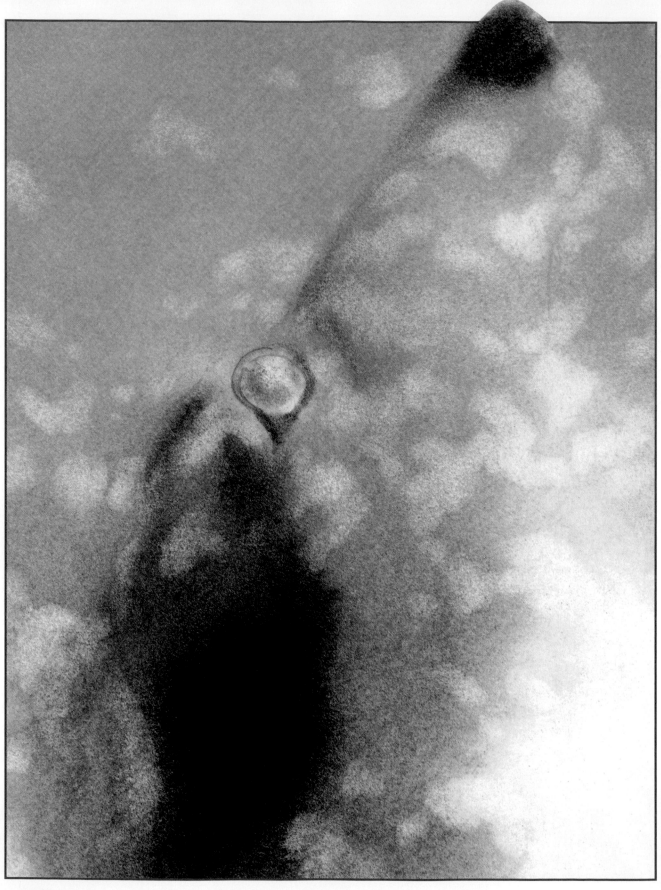

But when Shang stretched, she touched the wolf's tail. "Po Po, Po Po, your foot has a bush on it."

"Po Po has brought hemp strings to weave you a basket," the wolf said.

Shang touched grandmother's sharp claws. "Po Po, Po Po, your hand has thorns on it."

"Po Po has brought an awl to make shoes for you," the wolf said.

At once, Shang lit the light and the wolf blew it out again, but Shang had seen the wolf's hairy face.

"Po Po, Po Po," she said, for she was not only the eldest, she was the most clever, "you must be hungry. Have you eaten gingko nuts?"

"What is gingko?" the wolf asked.

"Gingko is soft and tender, like the skin of a baby. One taste and you will live forever," Shang said, "and the nuts grow on the top of the tree just outside the door."

The wolf gave a sigh. "Oh, dear. Po Po is old, her bones have become brittle. No longer can she climb trees."

"Good Po Po, we can pick some for you," Shang said.

The wolf was delighted.

Shang jumped out of bed and Tao and Paotze came with her to the gingko tree. There, Shang told her sisters about the wolf and all three climbed up the tall tree.

The wolf waited and waited. Plump Tao did not come back. Sweet Paotze did not come back. Shang did not come back, and no one brought any nuts from the gingko tree. At last the wolf shouted, "Where are you, children?"

"Po Po," Shang called out, "we are on the top of the tree eating gingko nuts."

"Good children," the wolf begged, "pluck some for me."

"But Po Po, gingko is magic only when it is plucked directly from the tree. You must come and pluck it from the tree yourself."

The wolf came outside and paced back and forth under the tree where he heard the three children eating the gingko nuts at the top. "Oh, Po Po, these nuts are so tasty! The skin so tender," Shang said. The wolf's mouth began to water for a taste.

Finally, Shang, the eldest and most clever child, said, "Po Po, Po Po, I have a plan. At the door there is a big basket. Behind it is a rope. Tie the rope to the basket, sit in the basket and throw the other end to me. I can pull you up."

The wolf was overjoyed and fetched the basket and the rope, then threw one end of the rope to the top of the tree. Shang caught the rope and began to pull the basket up and up.

Halfway she let go of the rope, and the basket and the wolf fell to the ground.

"I am so small and weak, Po Po," Shang pretended. "I could not hold the rope alone."

"This time I will help," Tao said. "Let us do it again."

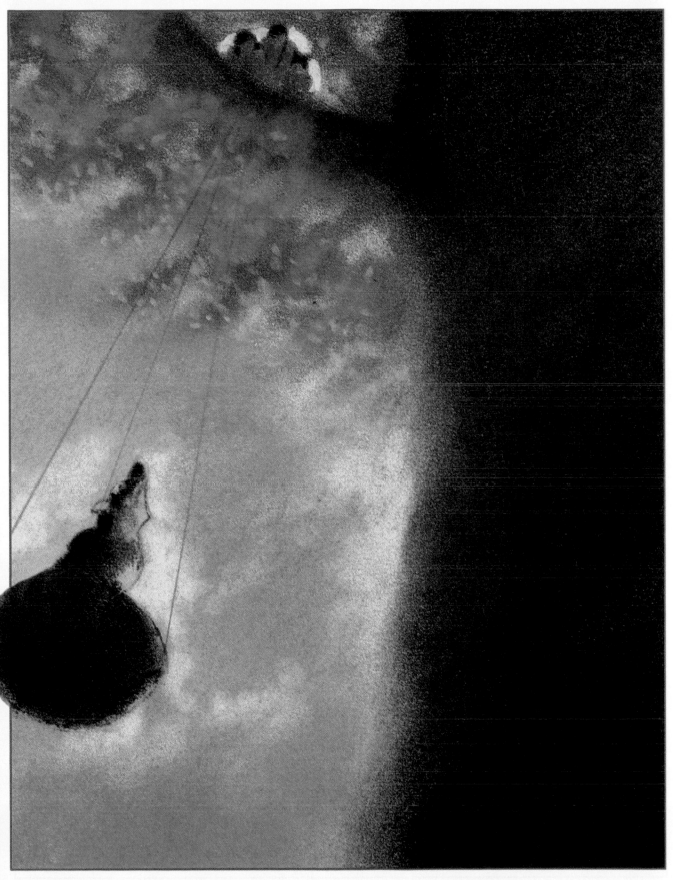

The wolf had only one thought in his mind: to taste a gingko nut. He climbed into the basket again. Now Shang and Tao pulled the rope on the basket together, higher and higher.

Again, they let go, and again the wolf tumbled down, down, and bumped his head.

The wolf was furious. He growled and cursed. "We could not hold the rope, Po Po," Shang said, "but only one gingko nut and you will be well again."

"I shall give a hand to my sisters this time," Paotze, the youngest, said. "This time we shall not fail."

Now the children pulled the rope with all of their strength. As they pulled they sang, "Hei yo, hei yo," and the basket rose straight up, higher than the first time, higher than the second time, higher and higher and higher until it nearly reached the top of the tree. When the wolf reached out, he could almost touch the highest branch.

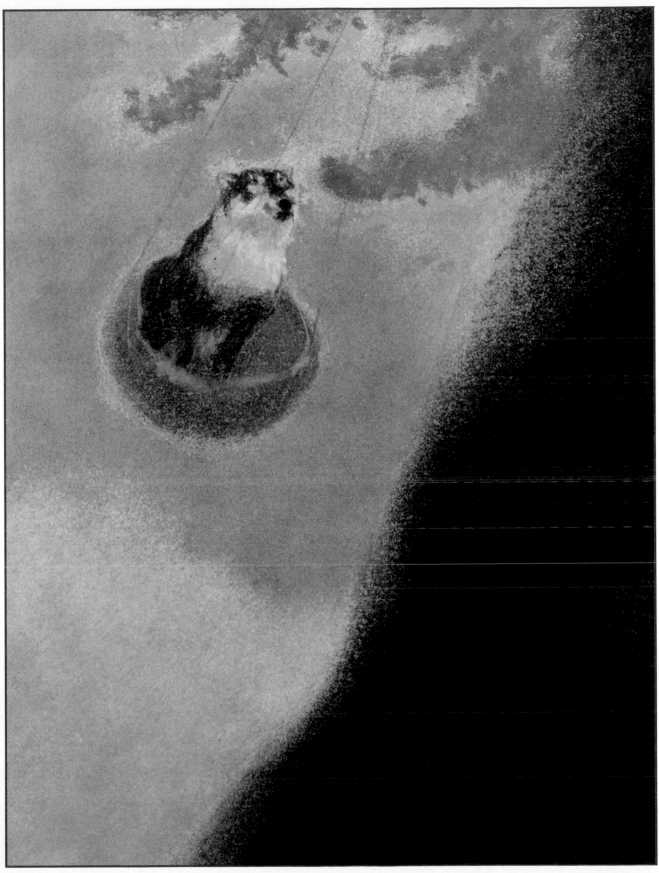

But at that moment, Shang coughed and they all let go of the rope, and the basket fell down and down and down. Not only did the wolf bump his head, but he broke his heart to pieces.

"Po Po," Shang shouted, but there was no answer.

"Po Po," Tao shouted, but there was no answer.

"Po Po," Paotze shouted. There was still no answer. The children climbed to the branches just above the wolf and saw that he was truly dead. Then they climbed down, went into the house, closed the door, locked the door with the latch and fell peacefully asleep.

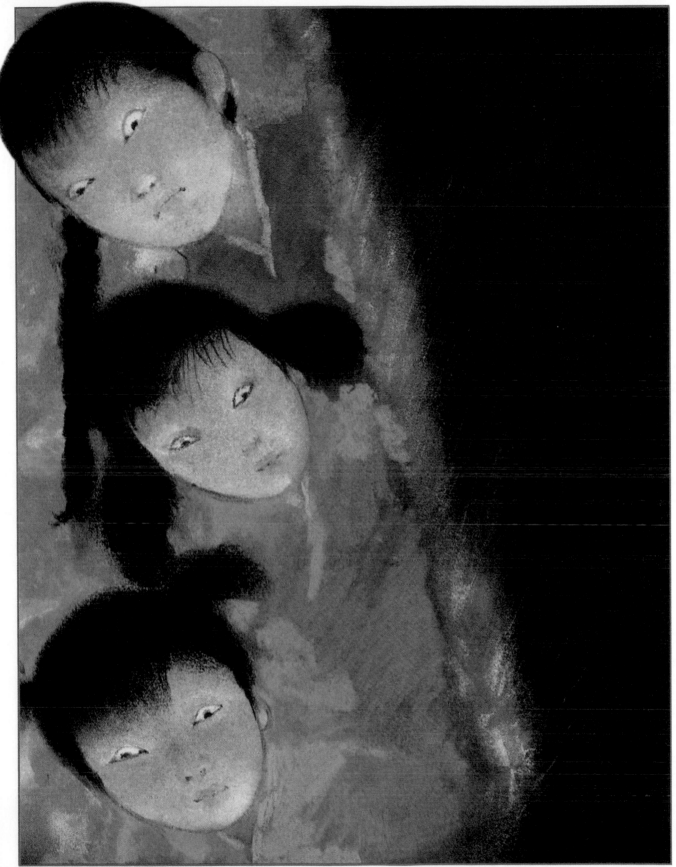

On the next day, their mother returned with baskets of food from their real Po Po, and the three sisters told her the story of the Po Po who had come.

Think and Respond

1 What happened to the sisters after their mother left to visit Po Po?

2 Why does Shang tell the wolf how **tender** and soft the gingko nuts are?

3 Do the children let go of the basket by accident or on purpose? How do you know?

4 What do you think the girls' mother will say when she hears their story?

5 What reading strategy helped you understand this story?

Meet the Author and Illustrator
Ed Young

Making the illustrations for *Lon Po Po* took some special thinking for artist Ed Young. To make his drawings look real, he had to learn about wolves. He also had to remember how children in China lived and even how trees grew there. Ed Young feels that if he learns everything he can about the people and places in a story, his drawings will make them real to others.

Ed Young thinks a story and its pictures need to work together to make a good book. "There are things that words can do that pictures never can," he says. He also thinks there are pictures that words can never describe. The words and pictures together can do what neither can do alone.

Making Connections

Compare Texts

1 Why does "Lon Po Po" belong in the theme Tell Me a Story?

2 How can you tell that Shang is suspicious of the wolf but her sisters are not?

3 If you did not know this was a Chinese tale, could you tell by reading it? Explain your answer.

4 How is "Lon Po Po" like "Little Red Riding Hood" and other fairy tales you know?

5 What lesson do you think Shang could share with others about home safety?

Write a Commercial

The wolf in "Lon Po Po" is eager to taste a gingko nut after Shang tells him how good they are. Think about how someone might try to sell gingko nuts in a television commercial. Write to persuade viewers to buy gingko nuts. Begin to plan your commercial by making a list of reasons you can use.

Writing CONNECTION

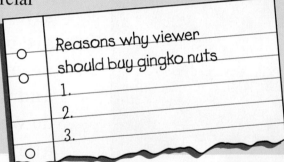

Reasons why viewer should buy gingko nuts
1.
2.
3.

Explain a Simple Machine

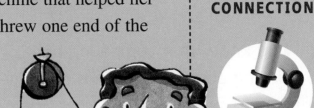

Shang created a simple machine that helped her lift a heavy load when she threw one end of the rope over a branch of the tree. Do research to find out about the six types of simple machines. Choose one simple machine to describe to your classmates. Use drawings or diagrams to show how the machine works.

Write a Report

A man named Marco Polo was one of the first Europeans to travel to China and learn of the great civilization there. Do research to find answers to these and other questions you may have:

- Who was Marco Polo? When and why did he travel to China?
- What did he do and learn in China?
- How did he share his knowledge of China with other Europeans?
- How did Marco Polo's travels affect Europe?

Write a report to share your information.

Compare and Contrast

You know that comparing and contrasting mean thinking about how things are alike and different.

In some ways, the stories "Lon Po Po" and "Little Red Riding Hood" are alike. In other ways, they are different.

	"Lon Po Po"	**"Little Red Riding Hood"**	**Both Stories**
Characters	three sisters	girl with red cape	wolf
Setting	China; in the country	in the woods	long ago
Plot	mother goes away wolf comes to door sisters trick wolf	girl goes to visit grand-mother girl figures out that wolf is trying to trick her	wolf pretends to be grand-mother happy ending

Visit *The Learning Site!*
www.harcourtschool.com

See *Skills* and *Activities*

116

Test Prep
Compare and Contrast

▶ **Compare the two stories to answer questions 1 and 2.**

Jack and Jill

Jack and Jill went up the hill
To fetch a pail of water.
Jack fell down
And broke his crown,
And Jill came tumbling after.

Joe and Jane

Joe and Jane were at the beach, building a big sand castle. They went to the water's edge and filled their pail. They carried it back together. Joe tripped, pulling Jane down with him. They fell on top of the castle and squashed it flat.

1. **The selections are different because "Jack and Jill"—**

   A tells a story

   B did not really happen

   C is told in rhyme

   D is about two children

Tip

The correct choice must be true only for "Jack and Jill."

2. **How are the selections alike?**

   F The characters have the same names.

   G Both have the same setting.

   H In both, the characters have a fall.

   J Both are about building sand castles.

Tip

Think about whether each choice is true and whether it tells a way the selections are alike.

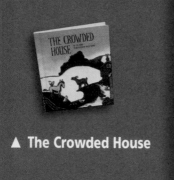

▲ **The Crowded House**

dreadful

wailing

wits

advice

faring

farewell

Vocabulary Power

What do you do when you don't know how to solve a problem? Everyone needs to ask for help at times.

We were walking to Uncle Ed's house on a **dreadful** day. As you can see, the weather was really bad. Suddenly we heard a terrible **wailing**. Where was that long, loud cry coming from? We were scared, but we kept our **wits** about us. We would need to be able to think clearly now.

We ran to Uncle Ed's house. We always ask his **advice**. He listens to us and helps us solve our problems.

We led Uncle Ed back to where we heard the wailing. We found a puppy that was stuck beneath a fence. Uncle Ed took the puppy home and named her Rainy Day. He decided to try and find her owner.

Later we had to say good-bye and wave **farewell** to Uncle Ed and Rainy Day.

She is **faring** much better now. We're happy that she's doing so well.

Vocabulary-Writing CONNECTION

Write an e-mail message in which you give a new student **advice** about doing well at your school.

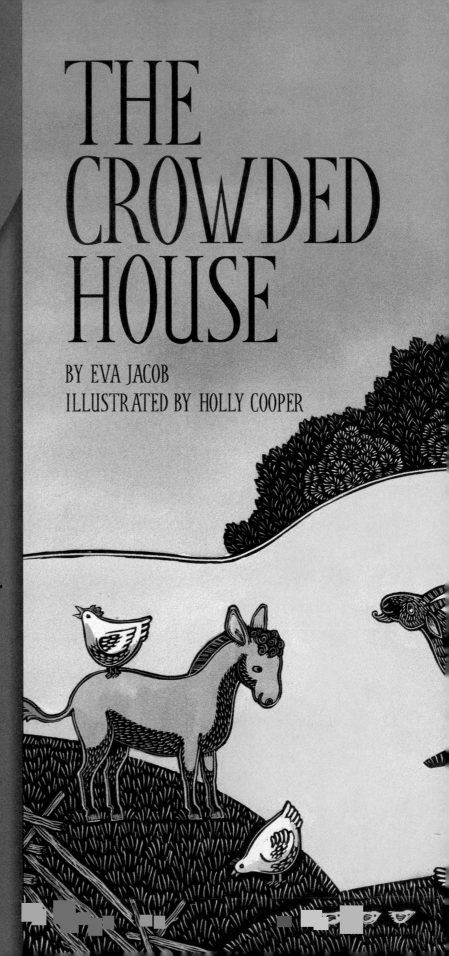

THE CROWDED HOUSE

BY EVA JACOB
ILLUSTRATED BY HOLLY COOPER

CHARACTERS

FATHER,
  John the Carpenter

MOTHER

MOLLY

JOAN

MEG

MARY ANN

MARTIN

WILLY

TOM

JOSEPH

GRANNY

BARTHOLOMEW,
  the Wise Man

GOAT

6 CHICKENS

DONKEY

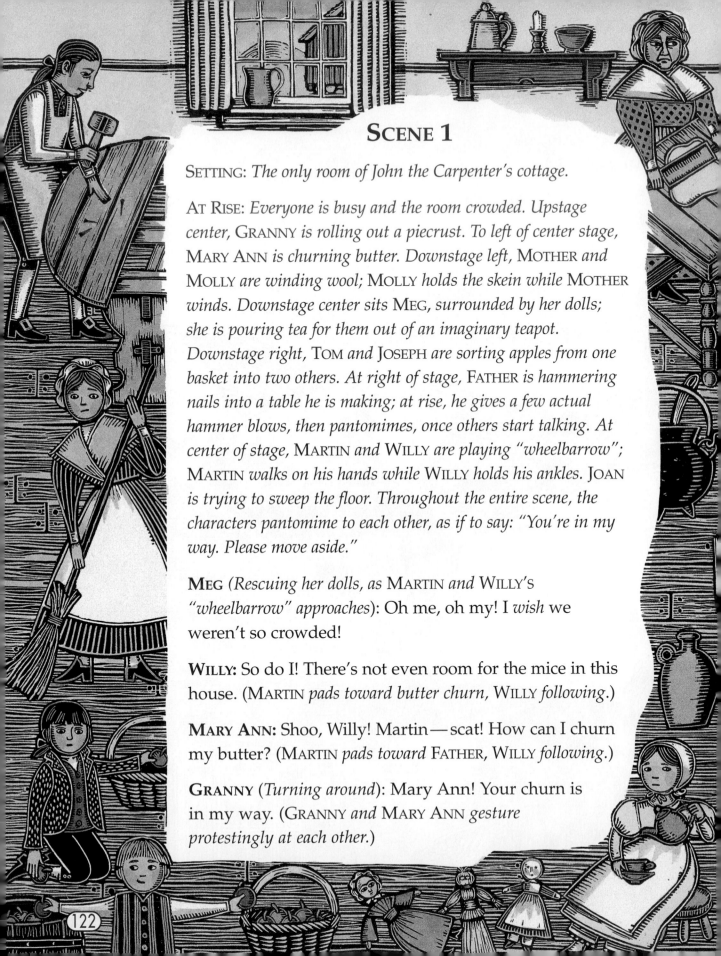

Scene 1

SETTING: *The only room of John the Carpenter's cottage.*

AT RISE: *Everyone is busy and the room crowded. Upstage center,* GRANNY *is rolling out a piecrust. To left of center stage,* MARY ANN *is churning butter. Downstage left,* MOTHER *and* MOLLY *are winding wool;* MOLLY *holds the skein while* MOTHER *winds. Downstage center sits* MEG, *surrounded by her dolls; she is pouring tea for them out of an imaginary teapot. Downstage right,* TOM *and* JOSEPH *are sorting apples from one basket into two others. At right of stage,* FATHER *is hammering nails into a table he is making; at rise, he gives a few actual hammer blows, then pantomimes, once others start talking. At center of stage,* MARTIN *and* WILLY *are playing "wheelbarrow";* MARTIN *walks on his hands while* WILLY *holds his ankles.* JOAN *is trying to sweep the floor. Throughout the entire scene, the characters pantomime to each other, as if to say: "You're in my way. Please move aside."*

MEG (*Rescuing her dolls, as* MARTIN *and* WILLY'S *"wheelbarrow" approaches*): Oh me, oh my! I *wish* we weren't so crowded!

WILLY: So do I! There's not even room for the mice in this house. (MARTIN *pads toward butter churn,* WILLY *following.*)

MARY ANN: Shoo, Willy! Martin—scat! How can I churn my butter? (MARTIN *pads toward* FATHER, WILLY *following.*)

GRANNY (*Turning around*): Mary Ann! Your churn is in my way. (GRANNY *and* MARY ANN *gesture protestingly at each other.*)

FATHER (*To* MARTIN *and* WILLY): Children, don't play here. There isn't any room.

JOAN (*Pausing with broom in front of apple baskets*): Joseph! Tom! Please move aside. How can I sweep? (BOYS *carrying baskets move angrily toward Meg.*)

MEG (*Again rescuing dolls*): No, Tom, you mustn't sit here. You're right in the middle of my tea party! (MEG, TOM, *and* JOSEPH *pantomime a quarrel. Others all begin talking at once.*)

ALL: You're in my way. Please move over. How can I work? There's no room in this house! Why must we be so crowded?

FATHER (*At the top of his lungs*): *Quiet!* Be still, I say. (*Others are silent.* FATHER *clutches his head.*) Oh my ears and shoe buttons! All this noise! You'll drive me out of my wits! (*A knock is heard at door left.*)

MOTHER: Husband, I hear a knock at the door. (*Knock is repeated.*)

FATHER: Aye, good wife. I hear it. (*Loudly*) Come in.

BARTHOLOMEW (*Entering. Leans on his staff and bows*): Good day to you, my friends.

GRANNY: Why, 'tis Wise Bartholomew himself!

BARTHOLOMEW (*Bowing again*): None other.

MOLLY: Have you come to visit us, good Bartholomew?

BARTHOLOMEW: Nay, my child. I was on my way to the forest, but I heard such a shouting and wailing in this house that I thought there must be some trouble.

MOTHER (*Wiping her eyes with her apron*): Alas, good Bartholomew, we have trouble enough and more.

FATHER: We lead a miserable life.

BARTHOLOMEW: Dear me! But what is the matter?

MEG: We're so *crowded*.

JOSEPH: We don't have any room at all.

ALL: He's in my way. She won't give me any room. How can I work? (*Etc.*)

BARTHOLOMEW (*Raising hand for silence*): Say no more. By all the gray hairs in my long gray beard, you really do have a problem.

FATHER: Dear Bartholomew, you are the wisest man in all the village. Can't you think of some way to help us?

OTHERS: Yes, please help us. There must be some way. Help us.

BARTHOLOMEW (*Again raising hand for silence*): Perhaps I can help you. Tell me this, friend John—do you own any animals?

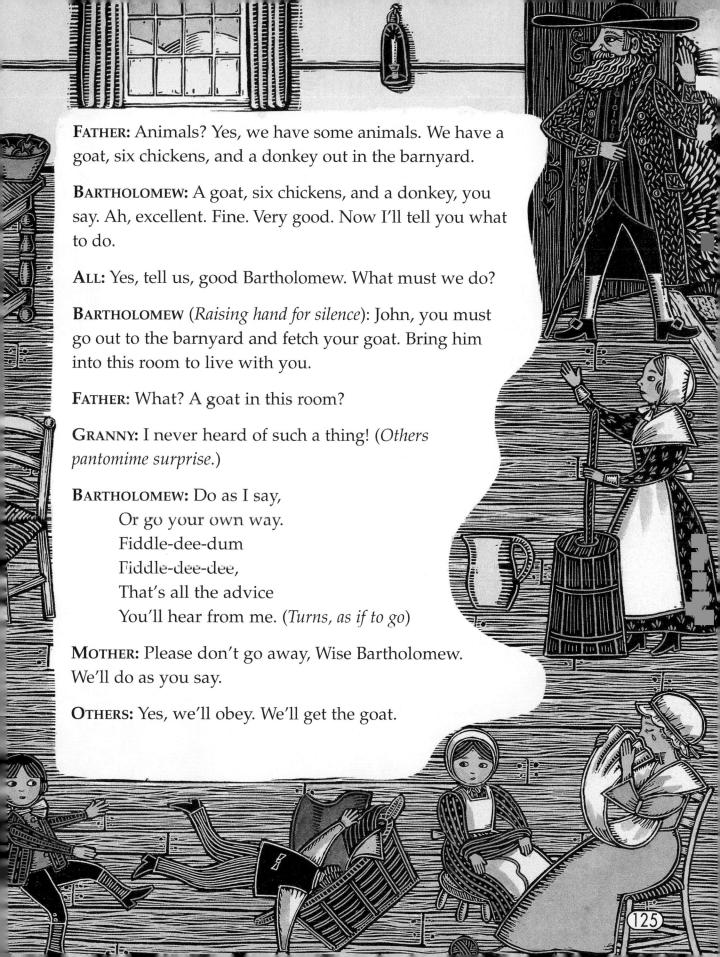

FATHER: Animals? Yes, we have some animals. We have a goat, six chickens, and a donkey out in the barnyard.

BARTHOLOMEW: A goat, six chickens, and a donkey, you say. Ah, excellent. Fine. Very good. Now I'll tell you what to do.

ALL: Yes, tell us, good Bartholomew. What must we do?

BARTHOLOMEW (*Raising hand for silence*): John, you must go out to the barnyard and fetch your goat. Bring him into this room to live with you.

FATHER: What? A goat in this room?

GRANNY: I never heard of such a thing! (*Others pantomime surprise.*)

BARTHOLOMEW: Do as I say,
    Or go your own way.
    Fiddle-dee-dum
    Fiddle-dee-dee,
    That's all the advice
    You'll hear from me. (*Turns, as if to go*)

MOTHER: Please don't go away, Wise Bartholomew. We'll do as you say.

OTHERS: Yes, we'll obey. We'll get the goat.

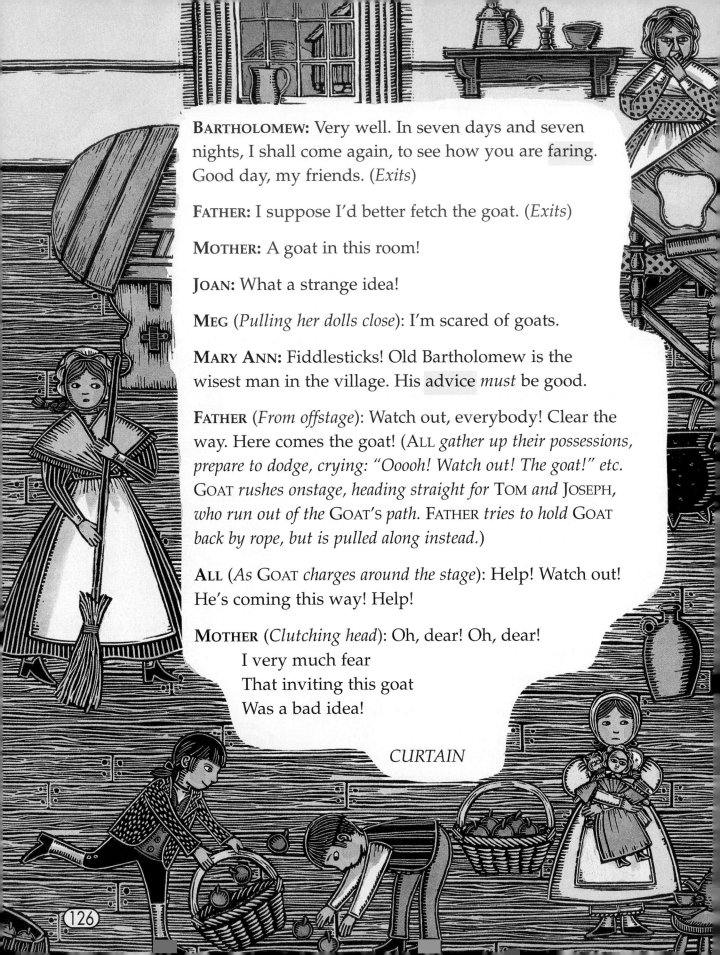

BARTHOLOMEW: Very well. In seven days and seven nights, I shall come again, to see how you are faring. Good day, my friends. (*Exits*)

FATHER: I suppose I'd better fetch the goat. (*Exits*)

MOTHER: A goat in this room!

JOAN: What a strange idea!

MEG (*Pulling her dolls close*): I'm scared of goats.

MARY ANN: Fiddlesticks! Old Bartholomew is the wisest man in the village. His advice *must* be good.

FATHER (*From offstage*): Watch out, everybody! Clear the way. Here comes the goat! (ALL *gather up their possessions, prepare to dodge, crying: "Ooooh! Watch out! The goat!" etc.* GOAT *rushes onstage, heading straight for* TOM *and* JOSEPH, *who run out of the* GOAT'S *path.* FATHER *tries to hold* GOAT *back by rope, but is pulled along instead.*)

ALL (*As* GOAT *charges around the stage*): Help! Watch out! He's coming this way! Help!

MOTHER (*Clutching head*): Oh, dear! Oh, dear!
    I very much fear
    That inviting this goat
    Was a bad idea!

CURTAIN

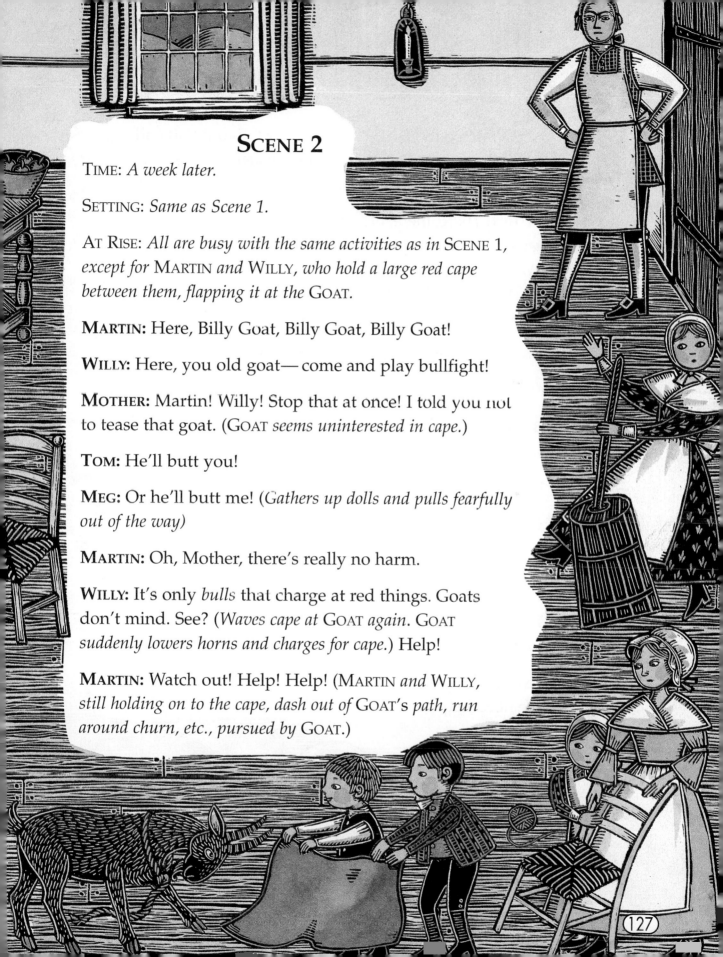

SCENE 2

TIME: *A week later.*

SETTING: *Same as Scene 1.*

AT RISE: *All are busy with the same activities as in* SCENE 1, *except for* MARTIN *and* WILLY, *who hold a large red cape between them, flapping it at the* GOAT.

MARTIN: Here, Billy Goat, Billy Goat, Billy Goat!

WILLY: Here, you old goat— come and play bullfight!

MOTHER: Martin! Willy! Stop that at once! I told you not to tease that goat. (GOAT *seems uninterested in cape.*)

TOM: He'll butt you!

MEG: Or he'll butt me! (*Gathers up dolls and pulls fearfully out of the way*)

MARTIN: Oh, Mother, there's really no harm.

WILLY: It's only *bulls* that charge at red things. Goats don't mind. See? (*Waves cape at* GOAT *again.* GOAT *suddenly lowers horns and charges for cape.*) Help!

MARTIN: Watch out! Help! Help! (MARTIN *and* WILLY, *still holding on to the cape, dash out of* GOAT's *path, run around churn, etc., pursued by* GOAT.)

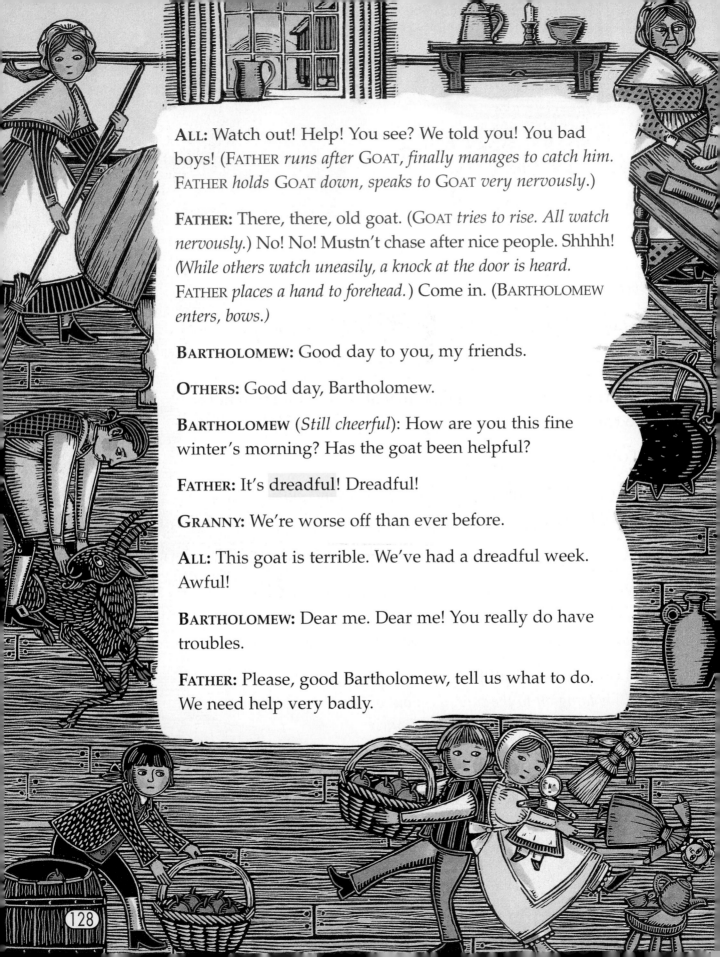

ALL: Watch out! Help! You see? We told you! You bad boys! (FATHER *runs after* GOAT, *finally manages to catch him.* FATHER *holds* GOAT *down, speaks to* GOAT *very nervously.*)

FATHER: There, there, old goat. (GOAT *tries to rise. All watch nervously.*) No! No! Mustn't chase after nice people. Shhhh! (*While others watch uneasily, a knock at the door is heard.* FATHER *places a hand to forehead.*) Come in. (BARTHOLOMEW *enters, bows.*)

BARTHOLOMEW: Good day to you, my friends.

OTHERS: Good day, Bartholomew.

BARTHOLOMEW (*Still cheerful*): How are you this fine winter's morning? Has the goat been helpful?

FATHER: It's dreadful! Dreadful!

GRANNY: We're worse off than ever before.

ALL: This goat is terrible. We've had a dreadful week. Awful!

BARTHOLOMEW: Dear me. Dear me! You really do have troubles.

FATHER: Please, good Bartholomew, tell us what to do. We need help very badly.

BARTHOLOMEW (*Stroking his beard*): Very well, friend John. This is what you must do. Go out to the barnyard and fetch your six chickens. Bring them into this room to live with you.

ALL: What? The chickens, too? Into this room?

BARTHOLOMEW: Do as I say,
　　　Or go your own way.
　　　Fiddle-dee-dum
　　　Fiddle-dee-dee,
　　　That's all the advice
　　　You'll hear from me. (*Turns, as if to go*)

MOTHER: Oh, dear! Oh, dear! Don't be angry, Bartholomew. We'll do as you say.

BARTHOLOMEW: Very well. In seven days and seven nights, I shall return to see how you are faring. Good day. (*Exits*)

GRANNY: Chickens!

MOLLY: The goat was bad enough!

FATHER: Old Bartholomew is the wisest man in the village. I think we should obey him. I'll go fetch the chickens. (*Exits*)

MOTHER (*Shaking her head*): Oh, dear! Oh, dear!
　　　I very much fear
　　　That we won't like having
　　　Those chickens in here.

CURTAIN

SCENE 3

TIME: *A week later.*

SETTING: *The same.*

AT RISE: *All are doing the same activities as before, but now they are more crowded than ever. The* GOAT *wanders around the stage, sniffing and butting everyone—and hopping, pecking, clucking everywhere are the* CHICKENS.

JOSEPH (*Shooing two* CHICKENS *away from his basket*): Shoo! Scat! (CHICKENS *squawk, flutter over to* MEG, *who shoos them away.*)

MARY ANN: Watch out for the goat!

MOTHER: Don't step on the chickens.

WILLY: Oh dear, I think I've stepped on an egg!

ALL (*Loudly, at once*): Shoo! Scat! Watch out! Keep that chicken away! Watch out for the goat! (*A knock is heard.*)

FATHER (*At the top of his lungs*): Quiet! (*Silence, except for* CHICKENS' *clucking*) I think I heard a knock. (*Knock is repeated.*) Come in.

BARTHOLOMEW (*Enters, bowing. Cheerily*): Good morrow to you, my friends. My, what lovely chickens!

MEG: They're not lovely—they're nasty!

ALL: They're awful! We're so crowded! We've had a terrible week! (CHICKENS *flutter about, clucking.*)

FATHER: Please, good Bartholomew. Help us.

MOTHER: We don't know *what* to do!

GRANNY: But, please, kind sir—no more goats and chickens!

BARTHOLOMEW: Very well, my friends. I'll tell you what to do. John, you must go out to the barnyard and fetch your *donkey*. Bring him into this room to live with you.

MOLLY: Oh, no! We *can't* do that!

TOM: Not the donkey, too!

BARTHOLOMEW: Fiddle-dee-dum
  Fiddle-dee-dee,
  That's all the advice
  You'll get from me.
  In seven days and seven nights, I shall return
  to see how you are faring. Good day, my friends.
  (*Exits*)

GRANNY: Well, I never!

MARY ANN: Don't do it, Papa! We *can't* live with a donkey!

FATHER: Old Bartholomew is the wisest man in all the village. (*Sighs*) Let's try his advice just one more time. I'll fetch the beast. (*Exits*)

MOTHER: The goat is a terror
  The hens are a brawl,
  But a donkey, I fear me,
  Is worst of them all.

CURTAIN

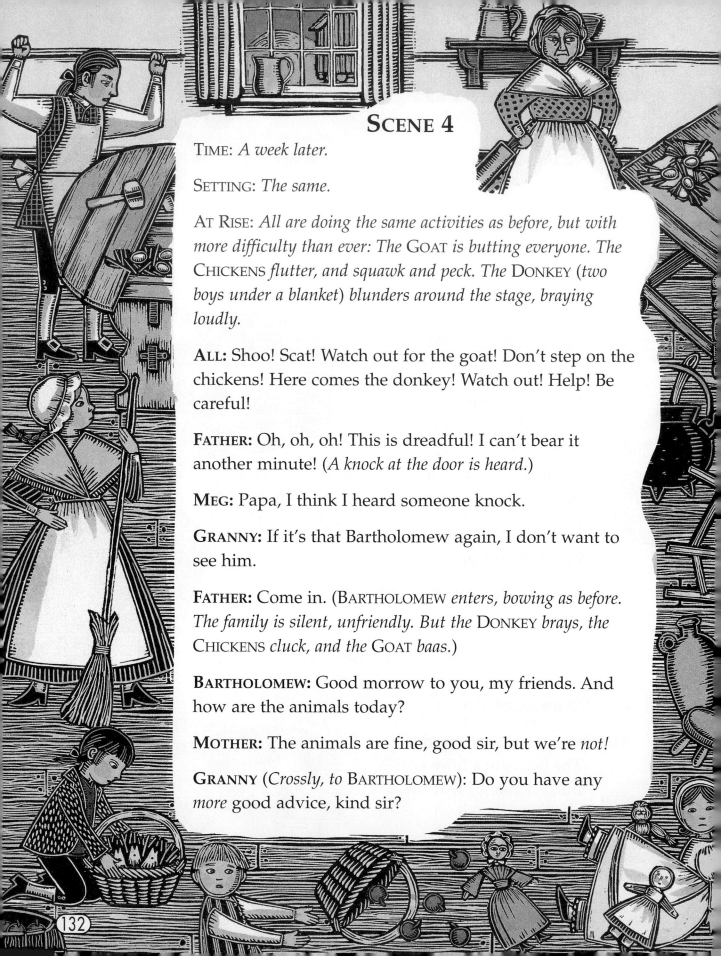

SCENE 4

TIME: *A week later.*

SETTING: *The same.*

AT RISE: *All are doing the same activities as before, but with more difficulty than ever: The* GOAT *is butting everyone. The* CHICKENS *flutter, and squawk and peck. The* DONKEY (*two boys under a blanket*) *blunders around the stage, braying loudly.*

ALL: Shoo! Scat! Watch out for the goat! Don't step on the chickens! Here comes the donkey! Watch out! Help! Be careful!

FATHER: Oh, oh, oh! This is dreadful! I can't bear it another minute! (*A knock at the door is heard.*)

MEG: Papa, I think I heard someone knock.

GRANNY: If it's that Bartholomew again, I don't want to see him.

FATHER: Come in. (BARTHOLOMEW *enters, bowing as before. The family is silent, unfriendly. But the* DONKEY *brays, the* CHICKENS *cluck, and the* GOAT *baas.*)

BARTHOLOMEW: Good morrow to you, my friends. And how are the animals today?

MOTHER: The animals are fine, good sir, but we're *not!*

GRANNY (*Crossly, to* BARTHOLOMEW): Do you have any *more* good advice, kind sir?

BARTHOLOMEW (*Still cheerful. Stroking his beard*):
Fiddle-dum, fiddle-dee; we'll see.

FATHER: Dear, good Bartholomew, you are still the
wisest man in all the village. *Please* help us. We've
never been so miserable.

BARTHOLOMEW (*Patting* DONKEY. *Looks up, as if astonished*):
Do you mean to say that you don't *like* these nice
animals?

JOAN (*Tartly*): Begging your pardon, sir, but you don't
have to live with them.

BARTHOLOMEW: You don't like living with them?

ALL: NO!

BARTHOLOMEW (*Stroking his beard*): Well now, there's
only one thing to do. John—

FATHER (*Fearfully*): Yes?

BARTHOLOMEW: Take all these animals—and put them
back in the barnyard where they belong!

ALL: Hurray! (JOHN *and others chase all the animals offstage
through the door; animals bray, cluck, and baa as they go off.*)

MOTHER: How wonderful! They're gone!

JOAN (*Puts broom aside. Stretches*): Mmmmm! Look at all
this room we have now. I'm *so* glad they're gone!

MARTIN: I really think this room has grown bigger.

GRANNY: I never knew before how nice it was *not* to have a donkey in the room.

MARY ANN: Or a goat.

WILLY: Or chickens.

TOM: Come on, Meg. Spread your silly dollies out. There's plenty of room now. (*All turn happily to their tasks.*)

MOLLY: It's so quiet and peaceful.

FATHER: I'm so happy. I never knew how much room we had!

BARTHOLOMEW: Fiddle-dum, fiddle-dee,
     As I've said thrice before:
     I don't think you'll be needing
     My advice any more.
     Farewell, my friends. (*Walks toward exit, waving.*)

ALL (*Waving*): Farewell, good Bartholomew! Farewell! Thank you! (*Curtain*)

THE END

Think and Respond

1 What is the family's problem? How does Bartholomew's **advice** help solve it?

2 What does the author of this play want you to learn?

3 Why do you think the author has Bartholomew speak in rhyme part of the time?

4 If your class were going to perform this play, which character would you want to be and why?

5 How did using reading strategies help you understand the play?

The Crowded House

A Yiddish Tale

retold by Pleasant deSpain
illustrated by Diane Paterson

Long ago there lived an unhappy man named Jacob. He lived in a tiny house with his wife, Leah, and their five children. The house was crowded!

The children played in every corner. Leah had little room for cooking and sewing. After a hard day of work in the fields, Jacob tried to rest by the fire in peace.

The house was noisy! The children yelled. Leah practiced her singing. Jacob couldn't hear himself think.

One day he went to the rabbi and asked for advice.

"I'm in a bad way," Jacob said. "My house is too small, and my family is too big.

The noise is making me crazy. What can I do?"

The rabbi thought and thought. Then he asked, "Do you have chickens in your front yard?"

"Yes," said Jacob. "We have seven chickens and one rooster."

"Move them into your house."

Jacob thought this strange, but he did as he was told.

A week later he returned to the rabbi, worse off than before.

"Help me, Rabbi. The chickens have taken over our house. They cluck and cluck and lay eggs in our beds. The rooster crows both day and night. My children can't sleep and Leah is upset. I'm so miserable."

The rabbi thought and thought. Then he asked, "Do you have a goat in the back yard?"

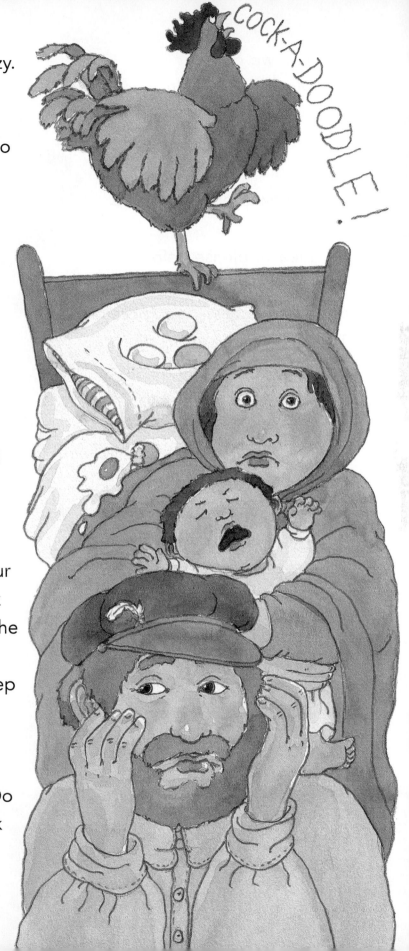

COCK-A-DOODLE!

"Yes, we do."

"Move the goat into your house."

Jacob thought this strange, but he did as he was told.

A week later he returned to the rabbi.

"Please, please help me, Rabbi. The goat knocks us about, and chews our socks. The chickens fly up to the rafters and drop feathers in our soup. The children scream and cry. Leah is angry. I'm going crazy. What should I do?"

The rabbi thought and thought. Then he asked, "Do you have a cow in the field?"

"Yes," said Jacob.

"Move the cow into your house."

Jacob thought this strange, but he did as he was told.

He returned to the rabbi one week later. His head hung down.

"Oh Rabbi, my life is ruined. The cow takes up so much room. She moos and chews all day long. The goat bleats. The chickens cluck and the rooster crows. My children shout, and Leah is *so* mad at me. What can I do?"

The rabbi thought and thought. Then he said, "Take the chickens and the rooster out of your house. Take the goat out of your house. Take the cow out of your house."

Jacob ran home and did as he was told.

One week later he went to see the rabbi.

"You are such a wise man," he said. "My house has so much room! The children play quietly. Leah is happy. I didn't know how peaceful life could be. Thank you, dear Rabbi, thank you."

Think and Respond

How do you know the rabbi is wise?

139

Making Connections

Compare Texts

1 Why do you think Eva Jacob decided to tell the story of "The Crowded House" as a play?

2 Which elements of the story stay the same from page to page? Which elements change?

3 What differences are there in story events and characters between the play and the folktale versions of "The Crowded House"?

4 What differences are there in the ways the story is presented in the play and in the folktale?

5 Do you think the family in the play will ask for Bartholomew's advice again? Why or why not?

Write a Friendly Letter

Imagine that you are a character in this play. Write a letter as that character to a friend, explaining what has happened. Write to tell about the events and to express the character's feelings and opinions. Use a graphic organizer like this one to plan your letter.

Writing CONNECTION

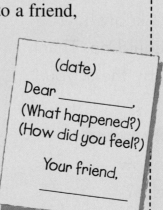

(date)

Dear _____,

(What happened?)
(How did you feel?)

Your friend,

_____

Create a Fact Sheet

In "The Crowded House," Mary Ann is churning butter. What does it mean to churn butter? How do we get products that are solid, such as butter and cheese, from liquid milk? What other products do we get from milk, and how are they manufactured? Use your information to create a dairy products fact sheet.

Science CONNECTION

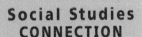

Create a Mural

No date is given for the setting of "The Crowded House," but the story probably takes place in the Middle Ages. Research what life was like for people in Europe in the Middle Ages. Look for information about

- what homes were like.
- what people did for a living.
- how people got food and clothing.

Then create a mural showing village life in the Middle Ages in Europe. Sketch your mural in pencil on a large sheet of paper, and then paint it.

Social Studies CONNECTION

Author's Purpose

Focus Skill

Recall what you have learned about the purposes an author may have for writing.

Author's Purpose

| to entertain | to inform | to persuade |

To identify Eva Jacob's purpose for writing the play "The Crowded House," think about what the play is like.

- It tells a funny story.

- It does not give facts.

- It does not try to get readers to do or believe something.

The author's purpose is to **entertain**.

If someone writes a newspaper article about road repairs, that author's purpose is to **inform**.

Visit *The Learning Site!*
www.harcourtschool.com

See *Skills* and *Activities*

If someone writes an advertisement to sell pet food, that author's purpose is to **persuade**.

Test Prep

Author's Purpose

▶ **Read each paragraph.**

> A   Goats make wonderful pets. They are very smart and
> playful. If you want a great pet, get yourself a goat.
>
> B   Did you know that we get wool from some types of goats?
> For example, the Kashmir goat of Asia has a special kind of
> fine wool called cashmere.

Now answer numbers 1 and 2. Base your answers on paragraphs A and B.

1. **What is the author's purpose in paragraph A?**

    A   to entertain

    B   to inform

    C   to tell how to do something

    D   to persuade

2. **Explain how you recognized the authors' different purposes in paragraphs A and B.**

Tip

Decide whether the author is telling a story, giving facts, telling how to do something, or suggesting what you should do or think.

Tip

Look at your answer to number 1. Tell briefly how you figured out the answer.

Good Neighbors

CONTENTS

▲ Leah's Pony

Vocabulary Power

county

auctioneer

bid

galloped

glistened

clutched

Good neighbors care about each other. These stories show some ways neighbors have helped each other.

Grandpa Moves In

Grandpa was moving in with us, but first he had to sell lots of furniture and old paintings. His neighbors helped him get ready. People came to the sale from all over the **county** and from other parts of the state, too.

An **auctioneer** was hired to run the sale. She asked people how much they would pay for each item. The person who made the highest **bid**, or offered the highest amount, got to buy the item. After the sale, Grandpa invited the neighbors to a picnic.

Mr. Baker's Horse

When I was young, my brother and I stopped every day to see Mr. Baker's horse. We watched it as it **galloped** at top speed around the field. Sometimes it stood quietly by the fence so we could pat it.

One day we saw our neighbor as he tried to brush the horse. He was having a hard time because he had a broken arm. We offered to help. We brushed the horse until its coat **glistened** and shone.

After his arm healed, Mr. Baker let us ride his horse. At first we **clutched** each other tightly to keep from falling off, but soon we felt at ease. We were glad we had offered help.

Vocabulary–Writing CONNECTION

Write a short one-act play. In the play, include an **auctioneer** and two other characters. Share your play with the group.

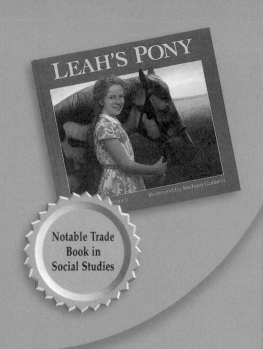

LEAH'S PONY

Illustrated by Michael Garland

Genre

Historical Fiction

Historical fiction is a story that is set in the past and portrays people, places, and events that did happen or could have happened.

In this selection, look for

- descriptive language that helps the reader understand the characters' feelings.

- a natural event that really happened.

Leah's Pony

by Elizabeth Friedrich
illustrated by
Michael Garland

The year the corn grew tall and straight, Leah's
papa bought her a pony. The pony was strong and swift
and sturdy, with just a snip of white at the end of his
soft black nose. Papa taught Leah to place her new saddle
right in the middle of his back and tighten the girth
around his belly, just so.

That whole summer, Leah and her pony crossed through cloud-capped cornfields and chased cattle through the pasture.

Leah scratched that special spot under her pony's mane and brushed him till his coat glistened like satin.

Each day Leah loved to ride her pony into town just to hear Mr. B. shout from the door of his grocery store, "That's the finest pony in the whole county."

The year the corn grew no taller than a man's thumb, Leah's house became very quiet. Sometimes on those hot, dry nights, Leah heard Papa and Mama's hushed voices whispering in the kitchen. She couldn't understand the words but knew their sad sound.

Some days the wind blew so hard it turned the sky black with dust. It was hard for Leah to keep her pony's coat shining. It was hard for Mama to keep the house clean. It was hard for Papa to carry buckets of water for the sow and her piglets.

Soon Papa sold the pigs and even some of the cattle. "These are hard times," he told Leah with a puzzled look. "That's what these days are, all right, hard times."

Mama used flour sacks to make underwear for Leah. Mama threw dishwater on her drooping petunias to keep them growing. And, no matter what else happened, Mama always woke Leah on Saturday with the smell of fresh, hot coffee cake baking.

One hot, dry, dusty day grasshoppers turned the day to night. They ate the trees bare and left only twigs behind.

The next day the neighbors filled their truck with all they owned and stopped to say good-bye. "We're off to Oregon," they said. "It must be better there." Papa, Mama, and Leah waved as their neighbors wobbled down the road in an old truck overflowing with chairs and bedsprings and wire.

The hot, dry, dusty days kept coming. On a day you could almost taste the earth in the air, Papa said, "I have something to tell you, Leah, and I want you to be brave. I borrowed money from the bank. I bought seeds, but the seeds dried up and blew away. Nothing grew. I don't have any corn to sell. Now I can't pay back the bank," Papa paused. "They're going to have an auction, Leah. They're going to sell the cattle and the chickens and the pickup truck."

Leah stared at Papa. His voice grew husky and soft. "Worst of all, they're going to sell my tractor. I'll never be able to plant corn when she's gone. Without my tractor, we might even have to leave the farm. I told you, Leah, these are hard times."

Leah knew what an auction meant. She knew eager faces with strange voices would come to their farm. They would stand outside and offer money for Papa's best bull and Mama's prize rooster and Leah's favorite calf.

All week Leah worried and waited and wondered what to do. One morning she watched as a man in a big hat hammered a sign into the ground in front of her house.

Leah wanted to run away. She raced her pony past empty fields lined with dry gullies. She galloped past a house with rags stuffed in broken windowpanes. She sped right past Mr. B. sweeping the steps outside his store.

At last Leah knew what she had to do. She turned her pony around and rode back into town. She stopped in front of Mr. B.'s store. "You can buy my pony," she said.

Mr. B. stopped sweeping and stared at her. "Why would you want to sell him?" he asked. "That's the finest pony in the county."

Leah swallowed hard. "I've grown a lot this summer," she said. "I'm getting too big for him."

Sunburned soil crunched under Leah's feet as she walked home alone. The auction had begun. Neighbors, friends, strangers—everyone clustered around the man in the big hat. "How much for this wagon?" boomed the man. "Five dollars. Ten dollars. Sold for fifteen dollars to the man in the green shirt."

Papa's best bull.

Sold.

Mama's prize rooster.

Sold.

Leah's favorite calf.

Sold.

Leah clutched her money in her hand. "It has to be enough," she whispered to herself. "It just has to be."

"Here's one of the best items in this entire auction," yelled the man in the big hat. "Who'll start the bidding at five hundred dollars for this practically new, all–purpose Farmall tractor? It'll plow, plant, fertilize, and even cultivate for you."

It was time. Leah's voice shook. "One dollar."

The man in the big hat laughed. "That's a low starting bid if I ever heard one," he said. "Now let's hear some serious bids."

No one moved. No one said a word. No one even seemed to breathe.

"Ladies and gentlemen, this tractor is a beauty! I have a bid of only one dollar for it. One dollar for this practically new Farmall tractor! Do I hear any other bids?"

Again no one moved. No one said a word. No one even seemed to breathe.

"This is ridiculous!" the man's voice boomed out from under his hat into the silence. "Sold to the young lady for one dollar."

The crowd cheered. Papa's mouth hung open. Mama cried. Leah proudly walked up and handed one dollar to the auctioneer in the big hat.

"That young lady bought one fine tractor for one very low price," the man continued. "Now how much am I bid for this flock of healthy young chickens?"

"I'll give you ten cents," offered a farmer who lived down the road.

"Ten cents! Ten cents is mighty cheap for a whole flock of chickens," the man said. His face looked angry.

Again no one moved. No one said a word. No one even seemed to breathe.

"Sold for ten cents!"

The farmer picked up the cage filled with chickens and walked over to Mama. "These chickens are yours," he said.

The man pushed his big hat back on his head. "How much for this good Ford pickup truck?" he asked.

"Twenty-five cents," yelled a neighbor from town.

Again no one moved. No one said a word. No one even seemed to breathe.

"Sold for twenty-five cents!" The man in the big hat shook his head. "This isn't supposed to be a penny auction!" he shouted.

The neighbor paid his twenty-five cents and took the keys to the pickup truck. "I think these will start your truck," he whispered as he dropped the keys into Papa's shirt pocket.

Leah watched as friends and neighbors bid a penny for a chicken or a nickel for a cow or a quarter for a plow. One by one, they gave everything back to Mama and Papa.

The crowds left. The sign disappeared. Chickens scratched in their coop, and cattle called for their corn. The farm was quiet. Too quiet. No familiar whinny greeted Leah when she entered the barn. Leah swallowed hard and straightened her back.

That night in Leah's hushed house, no sad voices whispered in the kitchen. Only Leah lay awake, listening to the clock chime nine and even ten times. Leah's heart seemed to copy its slow, sad beat.

The next morning Leah forced open the heavy barn doors to start her chores. A loud whinny greeted her. Leah ran and hugged the familiar furry neck and kissed the white snip of a nose. "You're back!" she cried. "How did you get here?"

Then Leah saw the note with her name written in big letters:

> Dear Leah,
>   This is the finest pony in the county. But he's a little bit small for me and a little bit big for my grandson.
>   He fits you much better.
>   Your friend,
>   Mr. B.
> P.S. I heard how you saved your family's farm. These hard times won't last forever.

And they didn't.

Think and Respond

1. How do Leah and her neighbors save the family's farm?

2. Why does Mr. B. give the pony back to Leah?

3. How do the people at the auction feel about Leah's **bid** of one dollar for the tractor? How can you tell?

4. Is Leah the kind of person you would like to have as a friend and neighbor? Explain your answer.

5. Give an example of a strategy you used as you were reading this story. Tell how this strategy was helpful.

Meet the Author

Readers can find out about new books by reading book reviews. A book review gives some information about the book, the author, and the illustrator. It also tells what the reviewer thinks of the book. This is what a book review might look like.

C-10 Friday, March 2   The Bigtown News

Leah's Pony a Delight

review by Maria Santos

"That's the best part about writing. It can take you anywhere!"

Leah's Pony is sure to please readers of all ages. The main character faces a choice between helping her family and keeping her pony. Children will understand how Leah feels about her difficult decision. Adults will find this warm, historical story interesting, too.

Author Elizabeth Friedrich loves to study history. She often wonders what it might have been like to live in another time. Her questions about the past led her to write this story about the Dust Bowl of the 1930s. "That's the best part about writing," she says. "It can take you anywhere!"

162

and the Illustrator
Elizabeth Friedrich
and Michael Garland

The Bigtown News

Friday, March 2 C-11

A picture book would not be complete without illustrations. The reader will find many beautiful paintings in *Leah's Pony*. Michael Garland did careful research to correctly show the cars, houses, and clothing of the 1930s. He even studied the work of Grant Wood, a well-known Midwestern artist of that time.

Garland used oil paints for the pictures in *Leah's Pony*. He is now creating some of his book art on a computer. "I'll still work in oils, but I'm eager to work on the computer," he says. He feels that the computer will make his work a little easier.

Together, Friedrich and Garland have created a book to remember!

"I'll still work in oils, but I'm eager to work on the computer."

**Visit *The Learning Site!*
www.harcourtschool.com**

Making Connections

Compare Texts

1 How do the people in Leah's community show that they are good neighbors?

2 When and why does the auction in "Leah's Pony" change from a regular auction into something else?

3 What happens that makes Leah's father fear he will lose the farm?

4 How does reading a historical fiction story like "Leah's Pony" help you understand the lives of real people who lived at that time?

5 Do you think Leah's family will be all right now? Why or why not?

Write a TV News Report

Think about what a TV news reporter might tell viewers about how Leah's farm was saved. Write to inform about the facts of this event. Use a graphic organizer like this one to plan your news report.

**Writing
CONNECTION**

Who took part in the event?

What happened?

When did it happen?

Where did it happen?

Why did the event take place?

Create a Booklet

Leah's family faces hard times when the corn her father plants does not grow. Corn has been grown in North America for at least 3,000 years and is the largest crop of the United States. Find out where and how corn grows and why it is such an important plant. Create a booklet that tells and shows some interesting information about corn.

Science CONNECTION

Make Question-and-Answer Cards

In "Leah's Pony," Leah lives on a farm. Different regions of the United States are used for farming, mining, manufacturing, or industry. Use sources to learn about the natural resources in your region. How are they used? How long will they last? Make a set of question-and-answer cards. Write a question on one side of the card and the answer on the other side. Quiz your classmates with the cards.

Social Studies CONNECTION

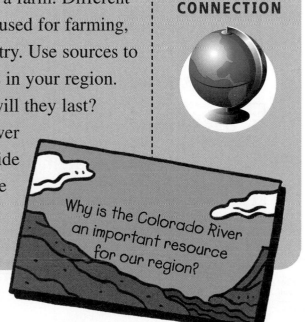

Why is the Colorado River an important resource for our region?

165

Fact and Opinion

Focus Skill

Some statements are facts. Others are opinions. A **fact** tells about something that can be seen or proved. It can tell what is happening or what has happened. An **opinion** is a person's thoughts or feelings. Often you can tell an opinion because it has signal words, such as *I think* or *I believe*.

Read these sentences from "Leah's Pony."

- Grasshoppers ate the trees bare and left only twigs behind.

- That's the finest pony in the whole county.

- She galloped past a house with rags stuffed in broken windowpanes.

- Here's one of the best items in this entire auction.

How can you tell which statements are facts and which are opinions? If you are not sure, ask yourself questions about it.

Is this something that can be proved?	Yes	No
If it is, then the statement is a fact.		
Is this what someone thinks or feels but cannot prove?	Yes	No
If it is, then the statement is an opinion.		

Visit *The Learning Site!* www.harcourtschool.com

See *Skills* and *Activities*

Test Prep
Fact and Opinion

Charlie's New Pony

Charlie has a new pony. Charlie's pony is a Shetland, which is the smallest kind of pony. She is just about 42 inches high at the shoulder.

I think Charlie's pony is beautiful. Her coat is brown and very pretty. Shetland ponies have thick coats because they come from the Shetland Islands, where the weather is often chilly and rainy.

Charlie is lucky to have such a sweet little pony. A pony is the best kind of pet.

Use "Charlie's New Pony" to answer questions 1 and 2.

1. **Which of these statements is a fact?**

   A   She is just about 42 inches high at the shoulder.

   B   Charlie's pony is beautiful.

   C   Her coat is very pretty.

   D   Charlie is lucky.

Tip

Read each statement. Ask yourself which one tells something that can be proved.

2. **Which of these statements is an opinion?**

   F   Charlie has a new pony.

   G   The Shetland is the smallest kind of pony.

   H   A pony is the best kind of pet.

   J   Shetland ponies come from the Shetland Islands.

Tip

Read each statement. Ask yourself which one tells what someone thinks or feels.

▲ Yippee-Yay!

Vocabulary Power

corral

ranchers

tending

stray

profit

market

Does "Yippee-Yay!" make you think of cowhands? Working on a ranch may sound like fun, but raising cattle is not an easy business.

Small ranch in trouble

*Ted Miller's cattle are in the **corral**, waiting to be sold.*

Ted Miller has owned a small cattle ranch for over thirty years. Like other **ranchers** in this area, he may soon have to sell his ranch.

"It's hard to find cowhands these days," Mr. Miller said.

"**Tending** cattle, looking after them, is hard work. Riding out in the rain or cold to find a **stray** steer that has wandered away isn't much fun. On some of the bigger ranches, they use airplanes and  helicopters for this, but those cost too much for me. I don't make enough **profit** for that. In other words, I don't have enough money left from the sale of my cattle after I pay the bills."

He pointed out his cattle that were waiting to be taken to **market**, where they would be sold. "This may be the last herd I raise," he said sadly.

Vocabulary–Writing CONNECTION

You have found a **stray** animal. What will you do? Write a short paragraph to describe the animal and what you might do to take care of it.

Yippee-Yay!
A Book about Cowboys and Cowgirls

ibbons

Award-Winning Author

Genre

Expository Nonfiction

Expository nonfiction explains information and ideas.

In this selection, look for

- **diagrams with labels.**
- **paragraphs with a main idea and supporting details.**

Yippee-Yay!

A BOOK ABOUT COWBOYS AND COWGIRLS

BY GAIL GIBBONS

COWGIRL

COWBOY

From the 1860s to the 1890s, the Old West was a rough and wild frontier. It was the era of the American cowboy. Not many women lived in the Old West, and there were only a few cowgirls. Besides, at that time, the work of a cowboy was considered too harsh for most women.

Wealthy ranchers owned large tracts of land on which they grazed longhorn cattle. These ranchers hired cowboys, whose lives centered around tending the cattle, rounding them up, and moving them on long cattle drives for sale and profit.

A cowboy's clothing was chosen for rough wear and tear. Many cowboys wore the same clothes for months at a time. Some even slept in them! Smelly and caked in dirt, these clothes were often burned after a long cattle drive.

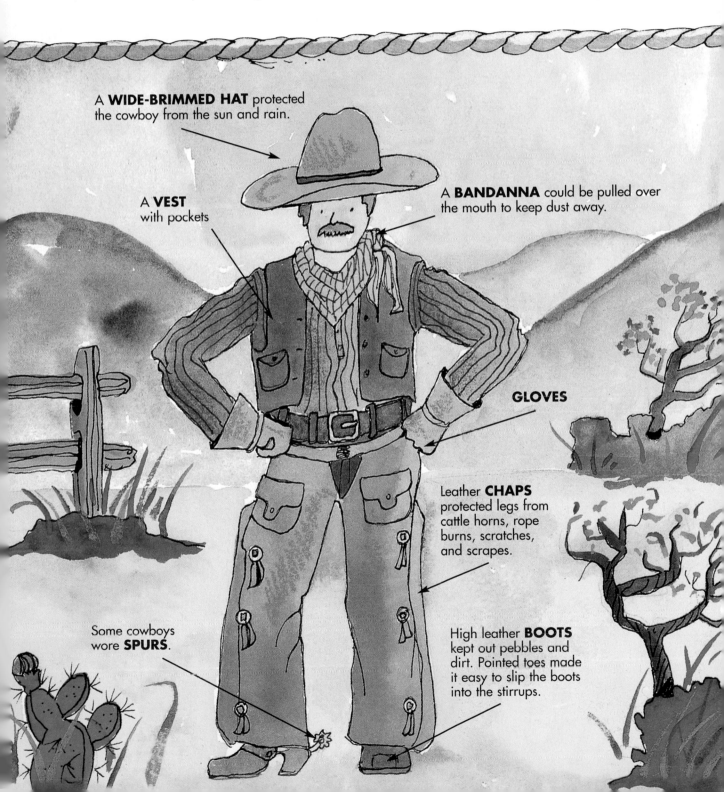

A **WIDE-BRIMMED HAT** protected the cowboy from the sun and rain.

A **VEST** with pockets

A **BANDANNA** could be pulled over the mouth to keep dust away.

GLOVES

Leather **CHAPS** protected legs from cattle horns, rope burns, scratches, and scrapes.

Some cowboys wore **SPURS**.

High leather **BOOTS** kept out pebbles and dirt. Pointed toes made it easy to slip the boots into the stirrups.

A cowboy could hold on to the **SADDLE HORN** and could also wrap one end of a rope around it while he was lassoing cattle.

The **CANTLE** supported the rider in the saddle.

A **BLANKET** kept the horse's back from getting sore.

The **STIRRUPS** held the cowboy's booted feet in place.

174

The **BRIDLE** controlled and guided the horse.

A cowboy's prized possession was his saddle. Without one, a cowboy couldn't work. The saddle had to be comfortable. Cowboys spent much of their time riding horses and ponies owned by the ranchers. Often the horse or pony became a cowboy's best partner.

Roping was the most difficult skill for a cowboy to learn, and it was the most important. Cowboys carried ropes called lariats to lasso cattle. It took many months of practice to learn to spin the lariat and release it at just the right moment.

LARIAT

A **BRONCO** is a partially tamed horse or pony that bucks.

BRONCOBUSTER

BUCKAROOS were assistants.

A **CORRAL** is a fenced-in area.

Wild horses had to be captured and tamed before they could work among the cattle. A skilled cowboy called a broncobuster would mount and ride the wild horse until it would trot obediently around the corral. What a wild ride! Busting, or breaking, horses was a very dangerous job.

Ranchers were unable to fence in the entire boundary of their many acres of land. So longhorns from different ranches would graze together freely. Once or twice a year, ranches held roundups. All the cattle and newborn calves would be rounded up, or brought to one location.

It was hard work to round up all those critters. Cattle are wild and fast. Any longhorn trying to get away would be lassoed and captured. The cowboy had a loop at the end of his lariat. When he twirled it and let it fly, the rope would snag the animal from afar. No cowboy wanted to get too close to an angry longhorn!

When the cattle were finally rounded up, the trail boss from each camp would count his herd. He could tell which longhorns belonged to his ranch by a mark on his cattle, called a brand. The calves didn't have brands. They were easy to identify because they followed their mothers.

Next, the cowboys lassoed the calves. This was called chopping out. One by one, the calves were brought to a wood fire filled with heated branding irons. The cowboys took turns pressing a branding iron to each calf's hip, leaving a mark.

Any stray steer within their own herd was lassoed, identified by its brand, and returned to the correct ranch. This was called cutting out.

Some common brands were

The Lazy J

The Flying V

The Scissors

The Quarter Circle T

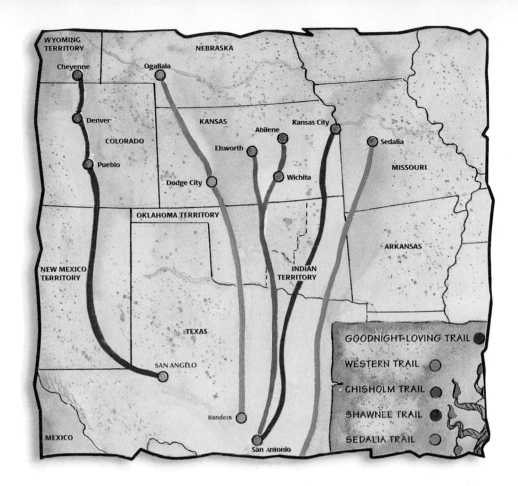

Cowboys who stole cattle from other ranches were called rustlers. These outlaws used a running iron to change the captured animals' brands to match their own. Pictures of rustlers' faces often appeared on wanted posters, and big rewards were promised for their arrest.

After the roundup came the trail drive. The best and the biggest longhorns would be moved in one huge herd along a trail to the closest town with a railroad station, called a railhead. The cattle were then brought to market by train.

Some trails were very long, nearly a thousand miles. Cowboys could drive the herd for only about ten to fifteen miles a day. They didn't want to push the cattle too hard, or they would lose weight, and they also took time to stop and let the animals graze along the way. Cattle drives could take many months. Only the toughest cowboys went on them.

A herd of several thousand cattle might stretch a mile along the trail and be tended by as many as fifteen cowboys. Each cowboy had his own task. The chuck wagon rolled along ahead of the herd, carrying food, cooking utensils, and bedding. Cowboys called food chuck. The chuck wagon was driven by the cook, called cookie.

Next came the wrangler. He was in charge of the spare horses, often numbering as many as one hundred. This group of horses was called a *remuda,* a Spanish word. The trail cowboys would switch to fresh horses three or four times a day.

The trail boss, also called the foreman, rode at the head of the herd. This cowboy had good knowledge of the trail, was able to communicate with the Native Americans they might encounter, and was an excellent tracker. As the cattle in the front of the herd began to move along, the other cattle followed.

REMUDA

WRANGLER

TRAIL BOSS
Also called the **FOREMAN**

POINT RIDER

The front of the herd was called the point position. The most experienced cowboys rode as point riders. They guided the steer in an arrowhead shape, keeping the pace and moving them along in the right direction. Cowboys called swing riders moved the herd forward and made sure the cattle didn't spread out too far.

The flank riders kept the cattle within the herd, preventing strays. The rear of the herd was called the drag position. The drag cowboys had the worst job of all. They rode through thick clouds of dust, urging slowpokes along and keeping an eye out for rustlers.

181

Some days the cowboys were in the saddle for sixteen hours—a long, hard day. Because the cookie traveled ahead with the chuck wagon, he was able to have food cooked and ready when the trail team arrived. A meal was usually pork and beans, sourdough bread, and coffee. "Come and get it!" he would call.

The cowboys often joked with the cookie while they ate their meal.

Many nights, cowboys would sit around the campfire, telling stories and singing old cowboy songs. It was a time to relax and gaze up at the never-ending sky filled with twinkling stars. Some cowhands used their saddles as pillows when they settled down in their bedrolls to sleep.

Day after day, the cattle moved along the dusty trail. What the cowboys feared most was a stampede. Cattle were easily spooked.

Oh, give me a home where the buffalo roam,
Where the deer and the antelope play,
Where seldom is heard a discouraging word,
And the skies are not cloudy all day.

Home, home on the range,
Where the deer and the antelope play,
Where seldom is heard a discouraging word,
And the skies are not cloudy all day.

Thunder and lightning or any strange noise could send the herd charging in a panic. It was the cowboys' job to get the herd back under control. Many cowboys were injured or killed carrying out this task.

After a long, hard journey, the cowboys and cattle at last made their way into town. The cowboys moved the cattle into pens near the railroad tracks. From there, the cattle would travel by train to points east. The rancher was paid for the steer, and the cowboys were paid for their work. It was time to have fun!

The first thing a cowboy wanted to do was soak in a hot tub. What a treat to get a haircut and a shave and to buy new clothes! The cowboys would then sing, dance, and have fun on the town. The sheriff always stayed nearby to be sure that law and order prevailed.

Back then, cowboys and cowgirls showed off their skills at rodeos—and they still do today. The word *rodeo* comes from the Spanish word *rodear,* meaning to encircle or round up. People in the stands cheer as cowboys and cowgirls compete for prizes.

Rodeos feature five main events: bronco riding, bull riding, bareback riding, steer wrestling, and calf roping. It's a colorful and rowdy scene!

Today, cowboys and cowgirls still tend cattle and have roundups. But the days of the long cattle drives are over. Railroads can now be found near almost every cattle ranch. Many cowhands have college degrees in agriculture and livestock breeding.

Cowhands drive pickup trucks and tractors and sometimes fly airplanes or helicopters to spot stray cattle. Cowboys and cowgirls today are still skilled in roping, branding, and riding horseback, just like the cowboys and cowgirls of the Old West.

Think and Respond

1. How are the lives of cowhands and **ranchers** of today different from those of long ago?

2. Why does the author label some of the illustrations?

3. Why did only the toughest cowhands go on trail drives?

4. What parts of being a cowhand would you most like and dIslike? Explain why.

5. Describe the strategies you used while reading this selection.

More Facts About Cowboys and Cowgirls

 The best-known cowboy hat is the Stetson, called the John B. after its maker, John B. Stetson.

 Cowboys in South America are called gauchos. In Chile, they are called *huasos,* and in England, drovers.

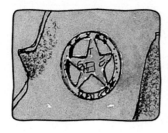 The Texas Rangers were formed in 1835 to deal with outlaws, cattle rustlers, and conflicts with Native Americans.

 The trail boss sometimes paid a toll to Native Americans when crossing their land. They paid as much as ten cents per steer or gave a few longhorns in trade.

 Between the 1860s and the 1890s, there were about forty thousand working cowboys and cowgirls.

 The American cowboy has always been a symbol of freedom and bravery.

Meet the Author and Illustrator
Gail Gibbons

Gail Gibbons has written more than sixty nonfiction books for children. We asked her about writing *Yippee-Yay!*

QUESTION: How did you become interested in learning about cowboys?

GAIL GIBBONS: A few years ago, I was at the Sonora Desert Museum in Arizona, doing research for another book. While I was there, I took a few side trips to some cattle ranches. I asked some librarian friends if there were any simple nonfiction books about cowboys and cowgirls. They said it would be wonderful if I wrote one.

QUESTION: What kind of research did you do for *Yippee-Yay!*?

GIBBONS: I talked to people at rodeos and people who run ranches. I also went to Tombstone, Arizona, to get the feeling of what a western town might have been like back in the Wild West days.

QUESTION: What is the most interesting fact about cowboys and cowgirls that you discovered in your research?

GIBBONS: The most interesting fact I learned was that on cattle drives each cowboy had a specific job to do. Cattle drives required team effort!

Visit *The Learning Site!*
www.harcourtschool.com

THIS LAND IS YOUR LAND

♪

words and music by Woody Guthrie

Trail Riders, **Thomas Hart Benton**
1964/1965. Polymer tempera on canvas 56 $\frac{1}{8}$ in. x 74 in. National Gallery of Art, Washington, D.C.

CHORUS

This land is your land,___ This land is my land,___ from Cal - i - for - nia___ to the New York is - land;___ From the red - wood for - est___ to the Gulf Stream wa - ters___

(to Verses) 1. This land was made for you and me.___

(Fine) me.___

As I was walking that ribbon of highway,
I saw above me that endless skyway;
I saw below me that golden valley:
This land was made for you and me.

I've roamed and rambled and I followed my footsteps
To the sparkling sands of her diamond deserts;
And all around me a voice was sounding:
This land was made for you and me.

When the sun came shining, and I was strolling,
And the wheat fields waving and the dust clouds rolling,
As the fog was lifting a voice was chanting:
This land was made for you and me.

Making Connections

Compare Texts

1 Why was it important for cowboys on a trail drive to get along with each other and do their jobs well?

2 How is the information on page 186 different from the information in the rest of the selection?

3 How are the feelings expressed in the song "This Land Is Your Land" like the feelings expressed in the cowboy song on page 182?

4 What is another informational book that you have read? Was the information in that book easier or more difficult to understand than the information in "Yippee-Yay!"? Explain your answer.

5 Now that you have read "Yippee-Yay!" what other questions might you ask about cattle ranching today?

Write an Opinion

Writing CONNECTION

"**Y**ippee-Yay!" describes what the different cowhands, such as the cook, the wrangler, and the trail boss, do on a trail drive. Write to explain which job you would prefer and why. Use a graphic organizer like this one to plan your paragraph.

Job I would like best:
Why I would like it:
1.
2.
3.

Draw Pictures

The cowboys in "Yippee-Yay!" sing "Oh, give me a home where the buffalo roam . . ." The Great Plains region of the United States was home to herds of buffalo. By 1900 they had almost disappeared. Do research to find out what happened to these animals and why the environment of the region changed. Draw a series of pictures with captions to show what happened to the buffalo during this period of time.

Science CONNECTION

Write a Report

"Yippee-Yay!" points out that the trail boss had to know how to communicate with Native Americans that the cowboys met. Research the first settlers in your own local region. How did the settlers affect Native Americans who already lived there? You may find information by visiting a local museum of natural history. Write a report to share with your classmates.

Social Studies CONNECTION

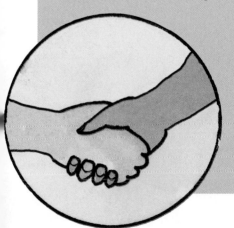

Main Idea and Details

The **main idea** is the most important idea of a passage or a selection. The main idea tells what a piece of writing is mostly about.

Details are facts that support the main idea by giving more information about it.

Look at the illustration on page 173. Use the web below to understand how the details give more information about the main idea.

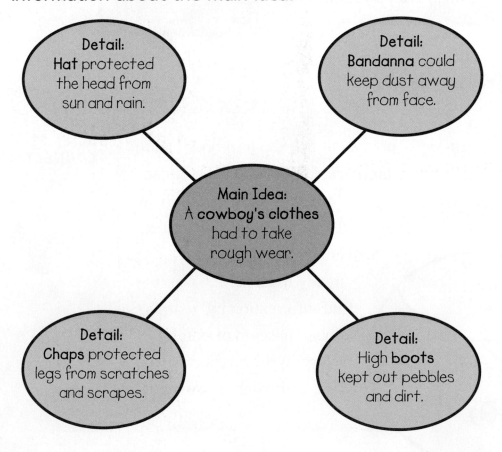

Detail:
Hat protected the head from sun and rain.

Detail:
Bandanna could keep dust away from face.

Main Idea:
A cowboy's clothes had to take rough wear.

Detail:
Chaps protected legs from scratches and scrapes.

Detail:
High **boots** kept out pebbles and dirt.

Test Prep
Main Idea and Details

▶ Read the paragraph and the list. Use them to help you answer Numbers 1 and 2.

> Firefighters wear special clothing to protect them on the job. They need to be safe from heat, flames, and smoke. They also need protection from objects that may fall on them in a burning building.
>
> - The *helmet* protects the firefighter's head from falling objects.
> - The knee-length *coat* is made of material that will not burn.
> - Special *pants* protect the firefighter's legs from heat and flames.
> - *Gloves* keep the firefighter's hands from being burned.
> - The *air cylinders* hold clean air for the firefighter to breathe.

1. What is the main idea of the paragraph?

   A Firefighters wear special boots.

   B Firefighters use gloves.

   C Firefighters work hard.

   D Firefighters are protected by special equipment.

Tip
Remember that the main idea tells the most important idea, or what the paragraph is mostly about.

2. Which of these details does not support the main idea?

   F The coat is knee-length.

   G The pants protect the legs.

   H A helmet protects the head.

   J Gloves protect the hands.

Tip
Reread your answer to number 1. Then decide which answer choice does not give more information about the main idea.

▲ Boom Town

boom town

miners

nuggets

settle

landmark

skillet

stagecoach

Vocabulary Power

Every town or city was once open, empty land. Do you wonder how our towns and cities got started and grew?

Our Own Boom Town

Our class went to the public library to see a show about the history of our town. I found out that it was a **boom town** many years ago. A boom town is a town that grows quickly. Many towns sprang up and grew fast in our part of the country when gold was discovered.

First came the **miners**, who worked at digging gold from the earth. They found **nuggets**, or lumps, of gold, but they couldn't eat them or wear them as jewelry. Soon other people saw a chance to start businesses. They earned money by selling the miners the things they needed. Then more people came to **settle** and make their homes here. The town grew larger and larger.

We saw some old pictures that showed how our town looked in those days. The old wooden church is one **landmark**, or outstanding building, that I was able to recognize. I was surprised to find out that another old building in town was once a general store. People could buy all kinds of things there—cloth, tools, eyeglasses, nails, rope, sugar, and eggs. They could even buy a **skillet** to fry their eggs in.

It's fun to imagine living in those days. It must have been exciting to ride on the **stagecoach**. The coach was pulled by horses. It traveled a route from town to town, carrying people, mail, and packages. Times have certainly changed!

Vocabulary–Writing CONNECTION

Write about a **landmark** in your city or town. Describe the building, when it was built, its importance, and its uses.

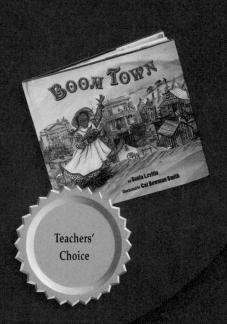

Historical Fiction

Historical fiction is a story that is set in the past and portrays people, places, and events that did happen or could have happened.

In this selection, look for

- the setting to be in a real time and place of the past.

- events that really happened.

Boom Town

by Sonia Levitin

illustrated by Cat Bowman Smith

It took us twenty-one days on the stagecoach to get to California. When we got there, I thought we'd live with Pa in the gold fields. A whole tent city was built up. But Ma shook her head. "The gold fields are no place for children. We'll get a cabin and live in town."

What town? A stage stop, a pump house, a few log cabins—that was all. It was so wide and lonesome out west, even my shadow ran off.

Ma found a cabin big enough for all of us: Baby Betsy, brothers Billy, Joe, Ted, and me—Amanda. Pa came in from the gold fields every Saturday night, singing:

"So I got a mule
And some mining tools,
A shovel and a pick and pan;

But I work all day
Without no pay.
I guess I'm a foolish man."

First Ma made him take a bath in a tin tub set out
under the stars. Then Pa sang songs and told stories
he'd heard from the miners—stories about men finding
big nuggets and striking it rich. But poor Pa, he had no
luck at all. Still, every Monday morning he'd leave for
the gold fields full of hope.

Days were long and lonely. The hills spread out as
far as forever. Nights, me and Ma and my brothers and
Baby Betsy would sit out and wait for a shooting star to
sail across the sky. Once in a while a crow flew by. That's
all the excitement there was.

My brothers worked up some furrows. They planted corn and potatoes and beans. Then they ran around climbing trees, skinning their knees. But after all the water was fetched and the wash was done, after the soap was made and the fire laid, after the beds were fixed and the floor was swept clean, I'd sit outside our cabin door with Baby Betsy, so bored I thought I'd die. Also, I hankered for some pie. I loved to bake pie.

I asked Ma and she said, "Pie would be good, but we have no pie pans and no real oven, just the wood stove. How would you bake a pie?"

I poked around in a big box of stuff and found an old iron skillet. I decided to make a pie crust and pick gooseberries to fill it.

Gooseberries grew on the bushes near town. I picked a big pailful and went back home. I made a crust with flour, butter, a little water, and a pinch of salt, and then I rolled it out.

Ma came in and said, "Looks good, Amanda. I knew you could make it. But tell me, how will you bake it?"

I showed Ma the skillet. She shook her head. "I don't think it will work, but you can try."

"It will work," I said.

Brothers Billy and Joe and Ted stood there laughing. When the wood turned to coals, I pushed my pie inside the old stove. After a while I smelled a bad burning. I pulled out my pie, hard as a rock. Billy, Joe, and Ted whooped and slapped their sides. They snatched up my pie and tossed it high into the air. They ran outside and Billy whacked it hard with a stick. Pie pieces flew all over the place, and my brothers bent over, laughing.

I was so mad I went right back in to make another, and I swore none of them would get a bite. I rolled out my crust and filled it with berries, shoved the pie into the oven, and soon took it out.

I set the pie down to cool. I went off to do some mending. Next thing I knew, Baby Betsy, just learning to walk, sat there with pie goo all over her face. Too soft, the filling ran down on Betsy, and she wailed like a coyote in the night.

It took one more try, but I got it right. That night we ate my gooseberry pie, and it was delicious.

When Pa came home from the gold fields on Saturday night, there was a pie for him, too. "Amanda, you are the queen of the kitchen!" Pa scooped me up and whirled me around. I was proud.

The next week I made an extra pie for Pa to take with him to the gold fields.

Saturday night when he came home singing, coins jangled in his pocket.

We all ran out to ask, "Did you strike gold, Pa?"

"No," he said. "I sold Amanda's pie. The miners loved it. They paid me twenty-five cents a slice!"

After that, Pa took pies to the gold fields every week. And every week he came home with coins in his pockets. Some miners walked right to our door looking for pie. They told Ma, "You should open a bakery."

Ma said, "It's my girl Amanda who is the baker. If she wants to make pies, that's fine. But I have no time."

Ma had a new baby on the way. It was up to me. I figured I could sell pies to the miners and fill up our money jar.

But I needed help. I rounded up my brothers and told them, "If you want to eat pie, you've got to work."

They grumbled and groaned, but they knew I meant it. So Billy built me a shelf, Joe made a sign, AMANDA'S FINE PIES, and Ted helped pick berries and sour apples.

I needed more pans and another bucket. One day Peddler Pete came by, and with the money I'd made I bought them.

"You're a right smart little girl," said the peddler, "being in business like this."

I thought fast and told him, "Anybody can make money out here. Folks need things all the time, and there're no stores around. If you were to settle and start one, I'll bet you'd get rich."

Peddler Pete scratched his beard. "Not a bad idea," he said. "My feet are sore from roaming. I could use this cart and build my way up to having a store."

So pretty soon we had a real store called PEDDLER PETE'S TRADING POST. Trappers and traders and travelers appeared. After shopping at Pete's, they were good and hungry.

They came to our cabin, looking for pie. Some liked it here so well they decided to stay. Soon we had a cooper, a tanner, a miller, a blacksmith. A town was starting to grow.

A prospector came in on the stage from St. Joe, his clothes covered with dirt. He looked around at the folks eating pie, and he asked, "Is there someone here who does washing?"

I stepped right up and I told him. "What we need is a laundry. Why don't you stay and start one? Why, the miners are sending their shirts clear to China. You'll make more money doing laundry than looking for gold."

The man thought a while, then said with a smile, "You're right, little lady. It's a dandy idea. I'll send for my wife to help."

Soon shirts and sheets fluttered on the line as people brought their washing in. A tailor came to make and mend clothes. A cobbler crafted shoes and boots. We heard the *tap tap* of his hammer and smelled the sweet leather. A barber moved in with shaving mugs, and an apothecary with herbs and healing drugs. So the town grew up all around us.

My pie business blossomed. Sometimes the line snaked clear around the house. Baby Betsy entertained the people while they waited. Billy added another shelf. Joe and Ted made a bench. We all picked berries and apples. Even Ma came to help. We had to get a bigger jar for all the money coming in.

One day our old friend Cowboy Charlie rode by. Like everyone else, he stopped for some pie. "I'd like to rest a spell," he said. "Where can I leave my horse for the night?"

"There's no livery stable," I said. "But why don't you start one? You'd rent out horses, and wagons too. That would be a perfect business for you."

"You're just full of great ideas, little lady," Cowboy Charlie said. He twirled his lariat. "I'd like to settle down. I'll stay here and do just that."

Soon a trail was worn right to Charlie's stable door. All day we heard the snorting of horses. Now Charlie needed hay. Farmers brought wagons and sacks full of feed. With all those people riding in, someone decided to build a hotel and a cafe. The town grew fast all around us.

The owner of the cafe bought pies from me, five or six at a time. I taught Billy how to roll the crust. Joe got wood for the stove. Ted washed the fruit, and Baby Betsy tried to stir in the sugar.

The money jar in our kitchen looked ready to bust. Where could we safely keep all that cash? Lucky us, one day Mr. Hooper, the banker, appeared.

"I'm building a bank," Mr. Hooper said to me. "This is getting to be a boom town."

"We'll use your bank," I told Mr. Hooper, "but the roads are so poor. In winter there's mud, and in summer there's dust. We need some sidewalks and better streets."

"You're a smart little lady," said Mr. Hooper, tipping his hat. "I'll see what I can do about that."

Before we knew it, the bank was built and wooden sidewalks were laid. One street was called Bank Street; the other was Main. Soon every lane and landmark had a name. Pa and my brothers built on a big room for our bakery.

Men sent for their families. New houses appeared everywhere. Babies and children filled up the town. We needed a school, and a good schoolmarm.

We knew Miss Camilla from our stagecoach days. She was living up the coast a ways. Cowboy Charlie rode off to fetch her, and she was glad to come.

Miss Camilla, the teacher, had married a preacher, and he came too. We all got together to build a church and a school. Bells rang out every day of the week. Now this was a real boom town!

One day Pa said to me, "Amanda, I'm through panning for gold. Will you let me be in business with you?"

"Sure!" I said, happily. "I'd love to work with you, Pa, and I'd also like to go to school."

So Pa turned to baking, and we all worked together. Pa sang while he rolled out the dough.

"Amanda found a skillet
and berries to fill it,
Made pies without a pan;

Our pies are the best
In all the West.
I guess I'm a lucky man."

Now Pa is with us every day. There's excitement and bustle all around. Our house sits in the middle of a boom town!
And to think it all started with me, Amanda, baking pies!

THINK AND RESPOND

1 How does Amanda help her town become a **boom town**?

2 How would you describe Amanda? How do you know what kind of person she is?

3 Why does Pa say he's a lucky man?

4 Would you have enjoyed living in Amanda's town in those days? Tell why or why not.

5 Give examples of some reading strategies you used while you were reading this story. How did they help you?

HISTORICAL NOTE

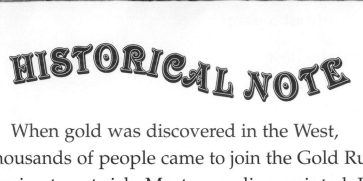

When gold was discovered in the West, thousands of people came to join the Gold Rush, hoping to get rich. Most were disappointed. It was not so easy to find gold. But many made fortunes by opening stores and providing things that the miners and their families needed.

"A young lady who learned to improvise baked $11,000 worth of pies in a small iron skillet." This book is dedicated to her and to all the resourceful and hardworking people who built the West.

Meet the Author
SONIA LEVITIN

Sonia Levitin loves the history of the West. She has read journals written by Western travelers during the late 1800s. These writings helped her understand how people lived during those times. She wrote three books about the Western frontier based on what she learned from them.

Boom Town is the second book of a series, a set of books that continue a story with the same characters. The first book, *Nine for California*, tells the story of Amanda's journey from Missouri to California. Amanda's adventures continue in the third book, *Taking Charge*.

Meet the Illustrator
CAT BOWMAN SMITH

Growing up, Cat Bowman Smith heard stories that were passed down in her family about frontier travel. She used these stories and her research to help her create the illustrations for Sonia Levitin's books. Her lively paintings capture what life was like in the old West. They also provide interesting facts about frontier times.

Our Nation's Oldest City
ST. AUGUSTINE, FLORIDA

St. Augustine's famous Bridge of Lions was built in 1927.

*C*an you imagine the United States before there were any cities? That is what the explorer Ponce de León saw in 1513. He had sailed from Spain and landed where St. Augustine, our nation's oldest city, now stands.

Cities are started when people who live near one another decide to work together and form their own local government. The people who start a city are called its *founders*. The founder of St. Augustine was Pedro Menéndez de Avilés. He named the city in 1565.

Most early cities in our country began as colonies. A colony is a settlement ruled by another country. St. Augustine was first ruled by Spain. Then, in 1763, England took over all of Florida. Many people came from England to build homes on the land.

St. Augustine grew steadily until 1836, but the native people were not happy with the changes caused by its growth. The people of the Seminole Indian tribe were forced to share their land with the new settlers. Eventually, a war broke out. This stopped the growth of the city for many years.

The Seminole War ended in 1841, but St. Augustine did not begin to develop again until the 1880s. The area became a popular vacation spot due to the mild weather. A wealthy man named Henry M. Flagler added to St. Augustine's growth by building a golf club and the Hotel Ponce de León. Flagler also built a hospital, the city hall, and several churches that are still in use today.

The oldest schoolhouse in the nation is still standing in St. Augustine.

Today, St. Augustine is home to more than 12,000 people. A city commission made up of five elected officials makes the rules for its citizens. The commission is led by a mayor. With good leadership and responsible citizens, the city of St. Augustine will continue to grow!

Think and Respond

Why do you think St. Augustine has succeeded as a city over so many years?

Making Connections

Compare Texts

1 How does the selection "Boom Town" fit into the theme Good Neighbors?

2 How do Amanda's brothers change their opinion of her pie-baking? How does the author show this change?

3 "Boom Town" and "Our Nation's Oldest City" both tell about places that grew into cities. How are the two selections different from each other?

4 In what ways are the selections "Boom Town" and "Leah's Pony" alike?

5 Which topic would you rather learn more about, gold mining or baking pies? What other topics from "Boom Town" might interest you?

Write a Paragraph That Contrasts

The town described in "Boom Town" changes a lot after Amanda comes to live there. Think about differences that the author describes. Write to contrast the town at the beginning of the story with the town at the end of the story. Use a graphic organizer like this one to plan your paragraph. You may add more contrasting details from the story if you wish.

Writing CONNECTION

Town at the Beginning	Town at the End
1.	
2.	
3.	

218

Write a Magazine Article

Amanda's father and the other miners came to the boom town to search for gold. Do research to find answers to these questions and other interesting facts about gold:

- Compared to other metals, is gold hard or soft?
- At what temperature does gold melt?
- At what temperature does gold boil and evaporate to become a gas?

Use your information to write and illustrate a short article for a children's science magazine.

Science CONNECTION

Create a Display

"Boom Town" tells how a community in California began and grew. When and why was your own community established? How did it grow and change over the years? Use primary sources such as newspapers, maps, letters, oral histories, and photographs to research the history of your town or city. Create a display to share historical information about your community.

Social Studies CONNECTION

"Main Street" 1900

Fact and Opinion

Focus Skill

A fact is something that can be proved.

An opinion is what someone thinks or feels. Other people may agree with an opinion. Some may disagree. An opinion does not have to be right or wrong.

FACT	Amanda tells Cowboy Charlie, "There's no livery stable."

OPINION	Amanda tells Cowboy Charlie, "That would be a perfect business for you."

Here are some other opinions about opening a livery stable.

A livery stable is just right for any cowboy.

I agree. I love horses.

I'd prefer Charlie to open a library. I like to read, and I don't need a stable.

An opinion may be shared by many people, but that doesn't make it a fact. Someone else might not feel the same way. It is still an opinion.

Visit *The Learning Site!*
www.harcourtschool.com

See *Skills and Activities*

Test Prep
Fact and Opinion

▶ Use "No Green Spaces" to answer questions 1 and 2.

No Green Spaces

I believe our town is growing too fast. New stores and office buildings are being built where there used to be green spaces. I think a town needs open spaces.

The shopping mall on Center Street is a good example. When my mother was a girl, that land was a green space with trees and a pond. Then the pond got filled in and built over. Now there is nothing there but a big, ugly mall.

1. *I think a town needs open spaces.*
   Is this a fact or an opinion?

   A It is a fact because it can be proved.

   B It is a fact because many people agree with it.

   C It is an opinion because it is not true.

   D It is an opinion because it is what someone thinks.

Tip

Decide whether the statement is a fact or an opinion, and think about why you decided as you did.

2. **Which of these statements is an opinion?**

   F New stores are being built.

   G Our town is growing too fast.

   H The pond got filled in.

   J The land was a green space.

Tip

Remember that an opinion tells what someone thinks or feels about something.

221

▲ Cocoa Ice

Vocabulary Power

schooner

trading

bargain

machete

harvest

pulp

support

Is it hot or cold where you live? What kinds of vegetables and fruits grow there? People have traveled all over the world to get different foods and other goods.

TRAVELING BY SCHOONER This kind of ship is called a **schooner**. It has two tall masts that hold up the sails. Years ago, schooners were **trading** ships. They sailed from one place to another to exchange goods. Because of traders, people were able to buy things from other places that they couldn't grow or make in their own

part of the world. To get a better price for items they wanted to buy or sell, people would sometimes **bargain**. When both sides were happy with what they were getting, an item was traded.

SUGARCANE This man is using a heavy knife called a **machete** to gather, or **harvest**, a crop. The plant he is cutting is sugarcane. Sugarcane grows in warm places. The sugar that is made from it is shipped all over the world.

WATERMELON Watermelons grow where summers are long and hot. Watermelons are dark green on the outside, but they have bright red or pink **pulp** on the inside. The pulp is soft, sweet, and juicy.

ICE SKATING In some parts of the world, winters are very cold. It gets so cold that the water in lakes and ponds turns to ice. The ice can be thick enough to **support**, or hold up, the weight of many people.

Vocabulary–Writing CONNECTION

Write a dialogue in which you and a friend bargain for something you each want.

Award-Winning
Author and
Illustrator

Informational Fiction

Informational fiction tells a story that explains a topic using characters and events that are not real.

In this selection, look for

- the importance of setting to a story.

- the information being given about a topic.

- characters and events that are usually realistic.

COCOA
ICE

By DIANA APPELBAUM
Pictures by HOLLY MEADE

COCOA

Chocolate comes from a faraway island where birds have pink feathers, leaves grow bigger than I am tall, and it is always summer. Children who live on the island never have to wear boots or clean ashes from the stove because winter never comes. Best of all on the island of always-summer, chocolate grows on trees.

The island where chocolate grows on trees is called Santo Domingo and I know all about it because Uncle Jacob sails there on a trading schooner. Once, he brought home a seashell for the mantel shelf. Inside, it is pink and smoother than anything in the world. If you hold it to your ear, it whispers, "Summer . . . summer . . . summer. . . ."

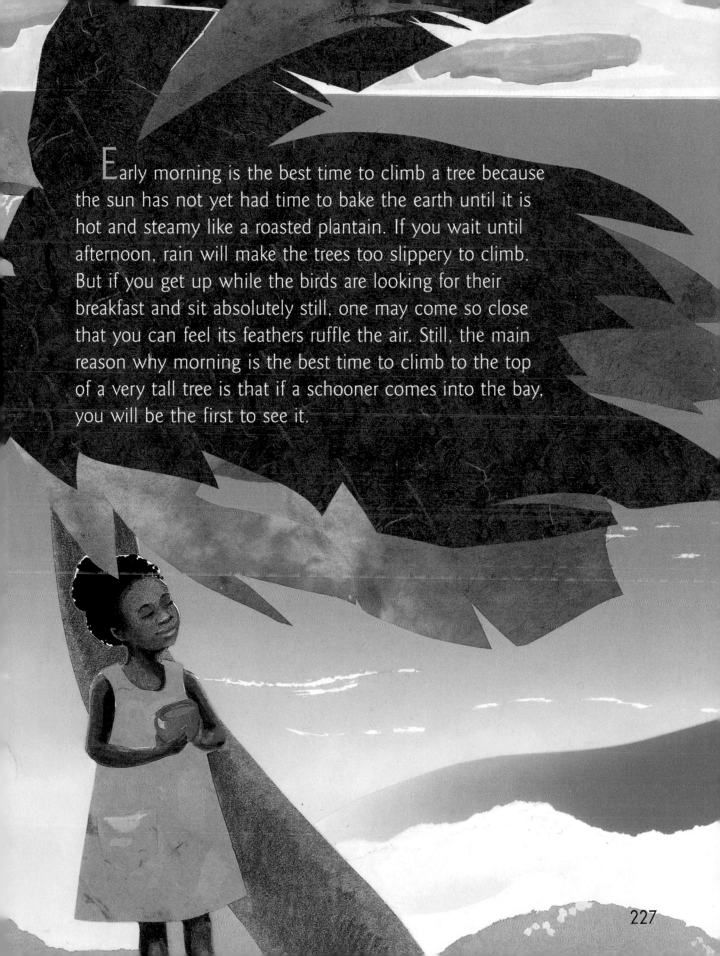

Early morning is the best time to climb a tree because the sun has not yet had time to bake the earth until it is hot and steamy like a roasted plantain. If you wait until afternoon, rain will make the trees too slippery to climb. But if you get up while the birds are looking for their breakfast and sit absolutely still, one may come so close that you can feel its feathers ruffle the air. Still, the main reason why morning is the best time to climb to the top of a very tall tree is that if a schooner comes into the bay, you will be the first to see it.

227

We have every kind of tree around our house: coconut, papaya, mango, orange, banana, plantain, breadfruit, guava, and a special kind called cacao—trees that grow chocolate. Cacao trees grow only in shade, so Papa plants young cacaos under tall banana trees that shade the growing cacao.

Little pink cacao flowers grow right on the trunk. Green cacao pods grow side by side with the flowers, and next to them grow ripe yellow and red pods, ready to be picked. A cacao tree is always blooming, always ripening, and always ready to harvest.

228

Papa splits the ripe cacao pods open with his machete and scoops out white pulp and pale beans. We spread slippery beans and sticky-sweet pulp on a carpet of banana leaves, then cover everything with more banana leaves.

I like to eat the sweet cacao pulp while we work, but I don't chew the beans! Once, I bit a fresh cocoa bean. It was so bitter it set my teeth on edge. Papa laughed and said, "Don't be so impatient, little one. Wait for the sun to make chocolate." And it does.

After a few hot days under the banana leaves, the pale, bitter cocoa beans begin to change color. We pick beans out of the old, smelly pulp and spread them to dry in the sun, turning them until they become a dark, beautiful brown.

Today the cocoa beans are drying. There is no work to do in the garden, and Papa says we are going conching. Mama wraps cassava bread in banana leaves and packs it in a basket with guavas for our lunch. It's hot paddling down the river San Juan, and we have a long way to go because after the river reaches the sea we must paddle along the beach until we reach a cove sheltered from ocean waves. I'm tired and thirsty when we finally pull the canoe onto the beach, so Papa opens coconuts and we drink their sweet milk. Now it is time to hunt for conchs.

I push my basket into the water and wade out until slippery leaves of turtle grass brush against my legs. Conchs are hiding in the turtle grass. Swimming slowly, I push the grass aside. Conchs look a lot like mossy rocks when they stand still, but I'll catch one if it hops.

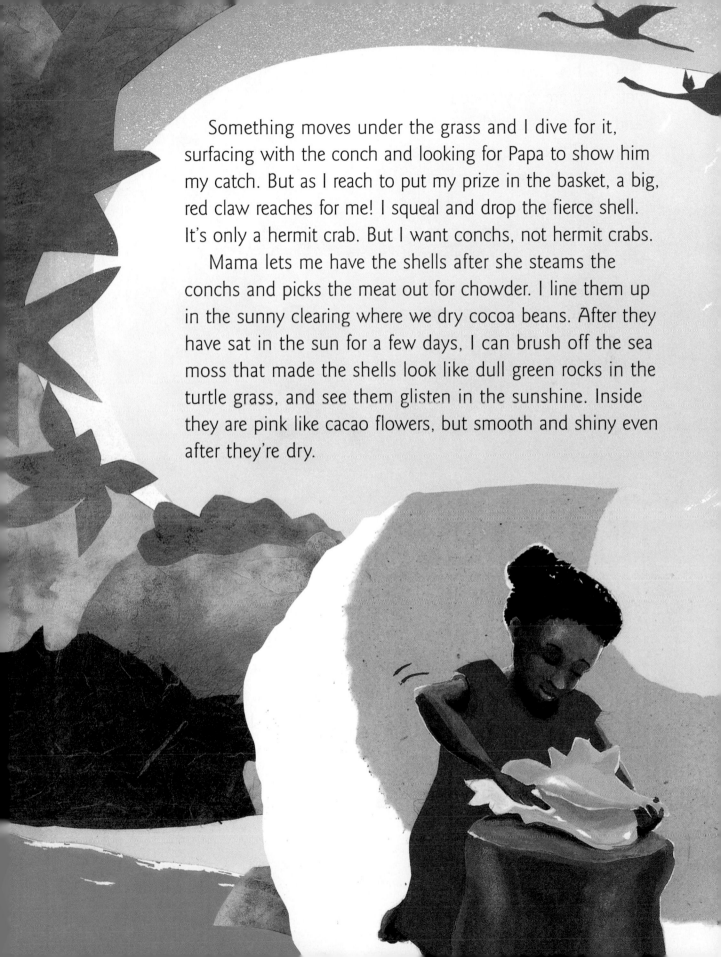

Something moves under the grass and I dive for it, surfacing with the conch and looking for Papa to show him my catch. But as I reach to put my prize in the basket, a big, red claw reaches for me! I squeal and drop the fierce shell. It's only a hermit crab. But I want conchs, not hermit crabs.

Mama lets me have the shells after she steams the conchs and picks the meat out for chowder. I line them up in the sunny clearing where we dry cocoa beans. After they have sat in the sun for a few days, I can brush off the sea moss that made the shells look like dull green rocks in the turtle grass, and see them glisten in the sunshine. Inside they are pink like cacao flowers, but smooth and shiny even after they're dry.

Our beans are not chocolate yet; they are only cocoa beans and we must turn them every day until they are dry. Mama roasts them over a hot fire until they begin to smell like chocolate. Then she lets me put them in the mortar and crush them. The best thing about being allowed to pound cocoa beans is the chocolate smell that curls up to your nose.

We put the crushed cocoa beans into a chocolate pot. While Mama boils the water, pours it over the beans, and adds sugar, I set out the cups. I think hot chocolate is the most wonderful drink in the whole world, unless there is an ice schooner in the bay.

When a schooner comes, Papa drags his canoe to the river. It took a long time to hollow the canoe out of a log, and Papa is very careful never to drag it over a rock.

We pile the sacks of dried cocoa beans into the canoe, along with a heap of coconuts and bananas. I climb in between two bunches of bananas as big as I am, settle my best conch shell between my feet, and we're on our way.

Papa carries me up the side of the ship on a rope, and one of the sailors leans down to lift me over the rail. Other families have come and Papa must wait his turn to trade with the captain. Clutching my conch shell, I search the crowd for the sailor named Jacob who once showed me pictures of his faraway country. He spots me first, and says hello with a big smile.

I show Jacob my beautiful conch shell and let him feel how smooth and pink it is inside. He shows me a picture of a girl, just my age, with a ribbon in her hair. Then he pulls a small, square bag with stitching on it from his pocket. Jacob holds the bag to his face, sniffs it, and smiles. I sniff too. It doesn't smell like chocolate or jasmine or papaya or anything in the world. It smells strange and wonderful. And now it's mine.

Papa trades too. I know he must bargain for a bolt of cloth, but I hop with pleasure when I see what else Papa has traded our cocoa beans for. ICE!

The sailors lower a block of ice into our canoe and Papa covers it with banana leaves. Then they hand me over the rail and, when I am settled, one of them passes down the new cloth. I put it carefully into a dry basket. Holding the bag with the wonderful smell safely in my lap, I wave good-bye to Jacob, the *marinero*.

When we get home, Mama scoops sweet, white pulp from a ripe cacao pod and beats it smooth and soft. Then she shaves the ice, stirs it into the cacao pulp, and pours it into cups for us to drink.

Cocoa ice is white and sweet and so cold I think it must be magic. It slides down my throat and makes me shiver to think of children living in such an icy place.

ICE

Ice schooners come from a land where the water is so hard that people walk on the river — right on the river. This place where water turns into ice is called Maine, and I know all about it because the sailor Jacob showed me pictures. In Maine the people build cooking fires inside their houses, and the trees don't have any leaves. And now I know another thing about Maine. I know that it has a wonderful smell. I sniff my balsam bag and try to imagine a land where children walk on rivers of ice.

Winter grips Maine hard. The days are short, bright, and so cold that sometimes nothing moves, not the wind, not the birds, not even the river.

But our kitchen is warm. Mama bakes apple pies in the big stove, and I practice my stitching by making a balsam pillow with fir needles. Papa and Uncle Jacob work for the ice company. If they can fill the big icehouses before spring breakup, Uncle Jacob's schooner and other ships can carry pieces of Maine winter to sell in hot countries far away. That's why we worry about snow.

Papa and Uncle Jacob and I stand on the riverbank stamping our boots, watching snow fall on new ice, and worrying.

"Figure it'll hold?" Papa asks, looking over the thin sheet of ice.

Uncle Jacob doesn't answer. They both know that air in the pockets of a million snowflakes will keep the river from freezing, and unless the river freezes there will be no ice to sell. But this ice is new and too thin to scrape. It has to be tapped—if it will hold the weight of a man.

We watch Uncle Jacob slide a wide plank onto the snowy surface and step out onto the river. It holds.

Soon a line of men follows Uncle Jacob. They inch forward, tapping holes in the ice with needle bars and mallets. River water seeps up through the holes, turning powder snow into a soggy slurry. If the weather stays cold, the icy water will freeze solid—thick enough to support a horse.

Horses are important once the ice is thick enough to scrape. After every snowstorm, Papa and Uncle Jacob harness our teams to heavy snow scrapers and clean snow off the river so the ice can freeze thick and clear. From Augusta all the way to Merrymeeting Bay, men and teams scrape snow to help the river freeze.

One morning when the sky is clear and there is no snow to scrape, Papa takes the wheels off the wagon box and puts the runners on. Mama bundles us in extra hats and mittens and tucks us into a pile of hay under a heavy quilt. Riding in a wagon on runners is like flying; we fly upriver clear to the falls! It's so cold that by morning the river has frozen more than a foot thick. Time to fill the icehouses.

I watch the ice boss rule a straight line across the river as though he were getting ready for a giant arithmetic lesson. Papa follows that line with the big ice cutter. The cutter's steel teeth slice through solid ice as easy as a knife slicing through Mama's apple pie, but Papa is careful not to cut through to the water. The ice has to stay solid enough to walk on until the whole surface has been grooved and cut into blocks. Back and forth they go, grooving and cutting until the river looks like a giant checkerboard, only—all the squares are white.

Fifty men are at work on the river today, grooving, cutting, sawing, and barring off blocks of ice, floating them across open water, pushing them into place on the elevator chain that lifts them toward the open door of the great icehouse. The upper doors are higher than the roof of the church, and the ice boss aims to fill it to the rafters before breakup.

I watch until I get so cold I have to run into the kitchen. Mama makes hot chocolate to warm me up.

Ice isn't worth anything unless you can get it all the way to summer without melting. That's why icehouse walls are built double, two walls with a wide space between, filled with sawdust to keep the cold in. That's why even icehouse doors are built double and filled with sawdust to keep summer out. And why we insulate the ice with a blanket of sweet meadow hay. When Uncle Jacob cuts the bales open, the green smell of summer meadows spills from the hay and fills the loft.

The men fill the great building one room at a time, lining blocks of ice up in perfect rows. Straight lines of ice that reach from wall to wall and rise in towers until they almost touch the roof. After the icehouse is full, the boss closes the doors and waits for the river to break up.

No matter how cold winter is, summer always comes. New grass in the pasture feels soft on my toes, and schooners come back up the Kennebec. Sailors fill the holds with ice, pouring a thick layer of sawdust all around as they stack it, and covering the sawdust with hay from our meadows.

Mama says ice from our river goes halfway around the world in ships that come home filled with silk and cashmere, ginger and tea. But the most important ship of all is the ice schooner Uncle Jacob is sailing on today, bound for Santo Domingo to bring home chocolate.

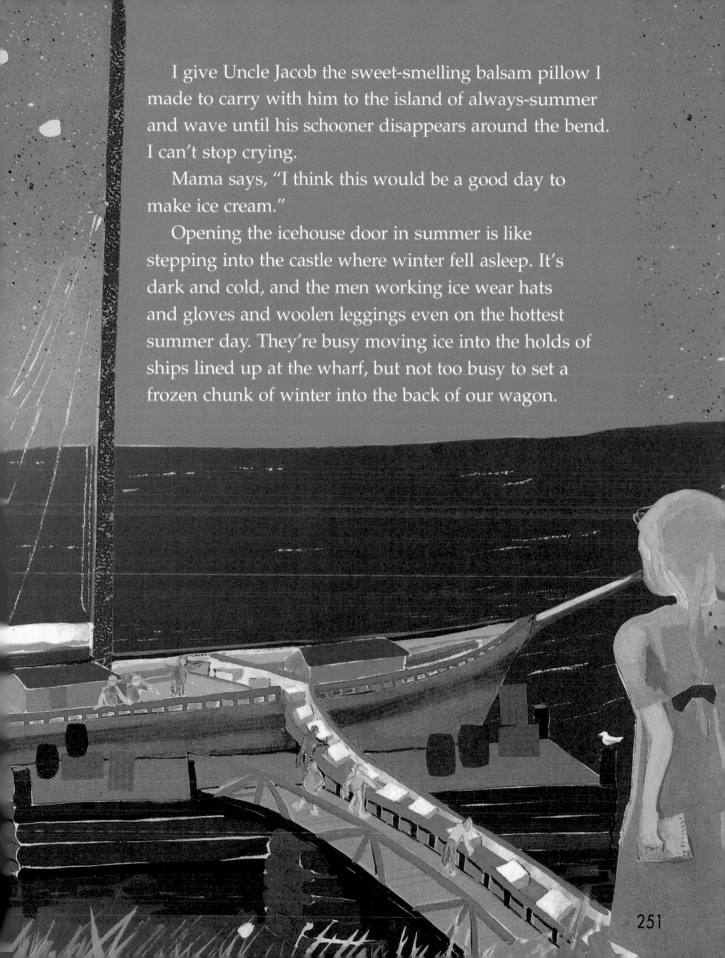

I give Uncle Jacob the sweet-smelling balsam pillow I made to carry with him to the island of always-summer and wave until his schooner disappears around the bend. I can't stop crying.

Mama says, "I think this would be a good day to make ice cream."

Opening the icehouse door in summer is like stepping into the castle where winter fell asleep. It's dark and cold, and the men working ice wear hats and gloves and woolen leggings even on the hottest summer day. They're busy moving ice into the holds of ships lined up at the wharf, but not too busy to set a frozen chunk of winter into the back of our wagon.

Mama measures cream and sugar into the can of the ice cream freezer while I carefully pour in the cocoa. Papa chips the ice and packs it around the can with layers of salt. Then I start to turn the crank. It turns easily at first, gentle strokes swirling chocolate, cream, and sugar round and round the dasher. But as the cream begins to freeze, my arm grows tired and the crank turns slow and slower until I can't turn it at all. Then Mama takes over and cranks until the ice cream is so hard the dasher won't turn another inch. When that happens, Mama sets the can on ice to keep until dinner and gives me the dasher to lick.

As I sit on the kitchen step licking chocolate from the ice-cold dasher, I close my eyes and imagine the island of always-summer, where giant pink seashells line the beaches and children pick chocolate from trees.

Think and Respond

1. Why are the **trading** ships important to the people in this story?

2. Why is Uncle Jacob an important character in this story?

3. Why is one of the illustrations for this fiction story a map?

4. Would you prefer to live in Santo Domingo or in Maine? Why?

5. What reading strategies did you use as you read this story? Give an example of how this helped you understand or enjoy the story.

253

Meet the Author
Diana Appelbaum

Diana Appelbaum lives in New England, where she studies and writes about history. As a child, Diana loved to read about real people. She enjoyed stories that told what life was like long ago for people all over the world.

Diana Appelbaum is now a historian. She does a lot of research about the past. Through her books, she shares with others the interesting things she learns. Diana Appelbaum feels that history is very important. "You can't understand the present unless you know about the past," she says.

Diane Appelbaum

Visit *The Learning Site!*
www.harcourtschool.com

Meet the Illustrator
Holly Meade

Holly Meade has been illustrating children's books since 1991. Before that, she worked as an artist for a magazine and a flag company. In 1997, the American Library Association awarded Holly Meade a Caldecott Honor for illustrating *Hush! A Thai Lullaby*. This award is given to some of the best illustrators of American picture books for children.

Holly Meade uses gouache, or watercolor paints, and cut or torn paper to create her artwork. Just as authors revise their stories, artists often have to change their illustrations several times. Holly Meade says that she makes hundreds of drawings for each picture book she illustrates.

"Working on *Cocoa Ice* was exciting," says Holly Meade. She found it a challenge to illustrate both a warm, tropical place and a cold, wintry place in the same book.

Holly Meade

WORK

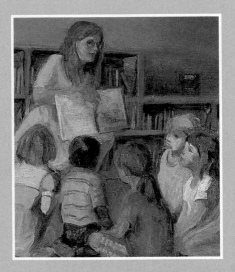

SONG

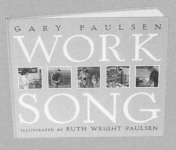

WRITTEN BY
GARY PAULSEN

ILLUSTRATED BY
RUTH WRIGHT
PAULSEN

Award-Winning
Author

It is keening noise and jolting sights,
and hammers flashing in the light,
and houses up and trees in sun,
and trucks on one more nighttime run.
It is fresh new food to fill the plates,
and flat, clean sidewalks to try to skate,
and towering buildings that were not there,
hanging suddenly in the air.
It is offices filled with glowing screens,
and workers making steel beams,
and ice-cream cones to lick and wear,
and all the pins that hold your hair.
It's gentle arms that lift and hold,
and all the soldiers brave and bold,
and help to fit the brand-new shoes,
and hands to show you books to use.
It is people here and people there,
making things for all to share;
all the things there are to be,
and nearly all there is to see.
And when the day is paid and done,
and all the errands have been run,
it's mother, father in a chair,
with tired eyes and loosened hair.
Resting short but loving long,
resting for the next day's song.

Making Connections

Compare Texts

1 What did you learn about communities by reading "Cocoa Ice"?

2 Why does the author divide the story into two different parts with the titles "Cocoa" and "Ice"?

3 How are the parents described in the poem "Worksong" like the parents of the two girls in "Cocoa Ice"?

4 What facts and events in "Cocoa Ice" do you think really happened? What events and details did the author make up?

5 What questions might you ask about the topic of schooners and other sailing vessels of long ago?

Write a How-to Guide

"Cocoa Ice" tells how cocoa beans are made into chocolate. Think of a food that is made in your home or community. Write to explain the steps in making this food. Use a graphic organizer like this one to plan your how-to guide. List as many steps as you need. You may also want to draw a picture to go with each step.

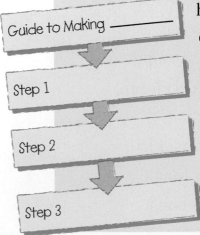

Guide to Making ———

Step 1

Step 2

Step 3

Writing CONNECTION

Make a Chart

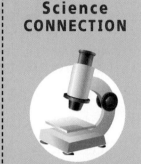

Cacao and conchs are found in Santo Domingo but not in Maine. Balsam fir trees grow in Maine but not in Santo Domingo. Go back to the story and find the names of other plants and animals that live in one place but not the other. Use encyclopedias, field guides, and other sources to add more examples to your list. Make a chart that lists plants and animals from each region. Add illustrations to your chart.

Santo Domingo		Maine	
Plants	Animals	Plants	Animals

Create a Three-Part Display

The people in "Cocoa Ice" traded goods for goods they could not grow or produce themselves. Think about the goods you use, such as food and clothing. Do research to find out where these items come from. Use words and pictures to create a three-part folding display. One part should show which goods are made or grown in your area. The second part should show goods that come from other parts of the United States. The third part should show goods received from other countries.

Compare and Contrast

There are two stories in "Cocoa Ice." One story is mostly about cocoa. The other is mostly about ice. Think about the characters, setting, and plot in both parts of "Cocoa Ice." How are they similar? How are they different?

Use the chart below to compare and contrast the settings in both parts of "Cocoa Ice." Write a few sentences to tell how Santo Domingo and Maine are alike and different.

COMPARE AND CONTRAST

	Santo Domingo	Maine
banana trees	✔	
balsam fir trees		✔
river	✔	✔
warm weather	✔	✔
cold weather		✔
an island	✔	
part of mainland		✔

Visit *The Learning Site!*
www.harcourtschool.com

See *Skills* and *Activities*

Test Prep
Compare and Contrast

Henry	Albert
Henry lives in Hawaii, where the weather is almost always warm. He loves surfing in the warm ocean waters. In school, Henry is learning about his state. He knows that its most important crops are sugarcane and pineapples.	Albert lives in Alaska, where the weather is often cold and snowy. He loves to ski on the snow and ice. In school, Albert is learning about his state. He knows that its important products include wood and petroleum.

Compare and contrast "Henry" and "Albert" to answer questions 1 and 2.

1. The stories are alike because—

    A the boys enjoy the same things

    B both have the same setting

    C they give the same kind of information

    D both are mostly about school

Tip

Decide whether each choice is true and whether it tells a way the stories are alike.

2. In both stories a boy—

    F likes warm water

    G watches a surfing contest

    H learns about his state

    J loves to ski

Tip

Compare the stories to decide which answer choice tells about both of them.

▲ If You Made
a Million

Vocabulary Power

choices

amount

value

combinations

receive

congratulations

Money is important. If your class needed to make money for a special reason, how might you help? Read about a class that decided to have a Spring Fair.

Record of Class Meetings
April 5
   Today we made plans for our Spring Fair. There were many ideas for different kinds of booths and games, so we had to make **choices**. We like the decisions we made. For each game or booth, we made a list of jobs that need to be done. We put the lists on the bulletin board so people can sign up for what they want to do.
   - Isaiah Barnes, recorder

April 12

*Some businesses in our neighborhood have given us a great **amount** of things to use for the fair. Although the number of things is large, none of the items have great **value**. They may not be worth much, but they will be very useful. We can use many of the items in different* **combinations**. *For example, we got some big boxes, boards, and paint. We plan to use all these items to make a giant dunk machine. We were very happy to* **receive** *these donations.*

- Ashley Anderson, recorder

April 19

Our Spring Fair was a great success! We made thirty-six dollars. Everyone is happy that we earned so much money. We had fun doing it, too.

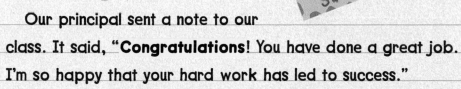

Our principal sent a note to our class. It said, "**Congratulations**! You have done a great job. I'm so happy that your hard work has led to success."

- Juan Santiago, recorder

Vocabulary-Writing CONNECTION

At special times, people offer their **congratulations**. Write a list of five events where you could give congratulations to a friend or relative.

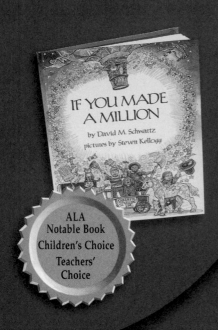

ALA
Notable Book
Children's Choice
Teachers'
Choice

If You Made a MILLION

by David M. Schwartz
pictures by Steven Kellogg

CHEERFUL AND WILLING
HELPERS
WANTED
by MARVELOSISSIMO
THE MATHEMATICAL MAGICIAN

CONGRATULATIONS!
YOU'VE EARNED A PENNY.

ONE PENNY

It will buy anything that costs one cent.

WELL DONE!
YOU'VE MADE A NICKEL.

ONE NICKEL

is worth the same as **FIVE PENNIES**

HOORAY!
NOW YOU HAVE A DIME.

ONE DIME

has the same value as **TWO NICKELS**

or **TEN PENNIES**

EXCELLENT!
FOR YOUR HARD WORK YOU'VE EARNED A QUARTER.

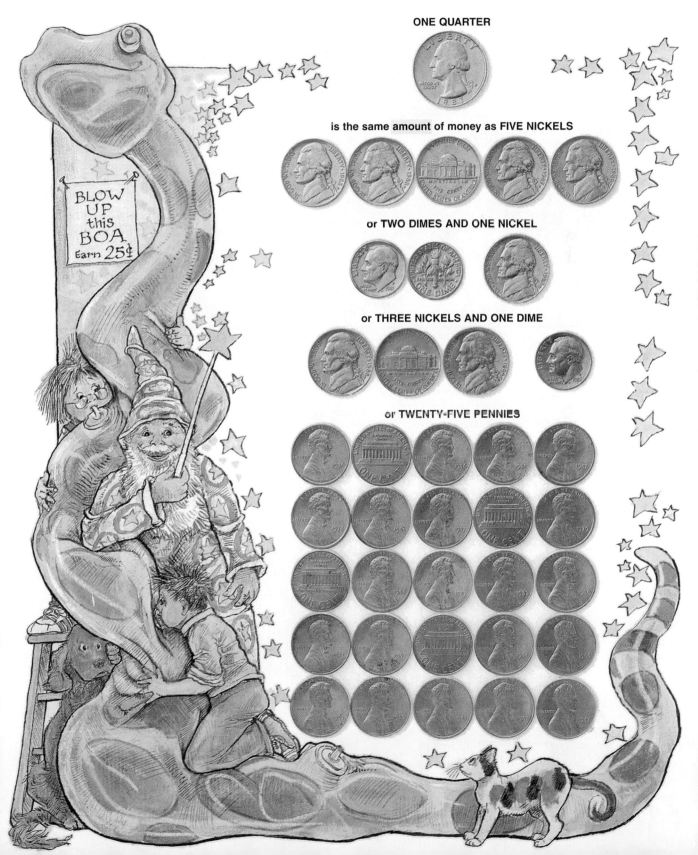

ONE QUARTER

is the same amount of money as **FIVE NICKELS**

or **TWO DIMES AND ONE NICKEL**

or **THREE NICKELS AND ONE DIME**

or **TWENTY-FIVE PENNIES**

BLOW
UP
this
BOA
Earn 25¢

WONDERFUL!
YOU ARE NOW A DOLLAR RICHER.

ONE DOLLAR

is worth as much as FOUR QUARTERS

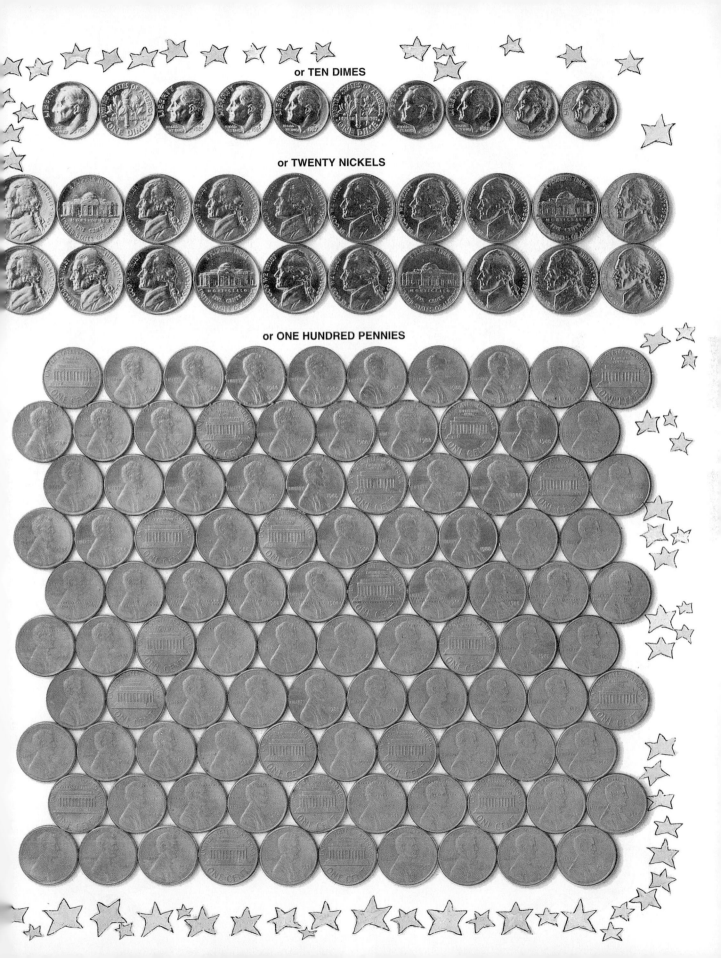

or TEN DIMES

or TWENTY NICKELS

or ONE HUNDRED PENNIES

You could use your dollar to buy one hundred
pieces of penny candy, or twenty five-cent balloons,

270

or ten stickers for ten cents each, or four rubber balls that cost twenty-five cents apiece.

Or perhaps you'd like to save your dollar. You could put it in the bank, and a year from now it will be worth $1.05.

The bank wants to use your money, and it will pay you five cents to leave your dollar there for a year. The extra five cents is called interest.

If you waited ten years, your dollar would earn
sixty-four cents in interest just from sitting in the bank.

Are you interested in earning lots of interest?
Wait twenty years, and one dollar will grow to $2.70.

DELICIOUS!
YOU'VE BAKED A CAKE AND EARNED FIVE DOLLARS.

You could be paid with one five-dollar bill or five
one-dollar bills. It doesn't matter. They have the same value.

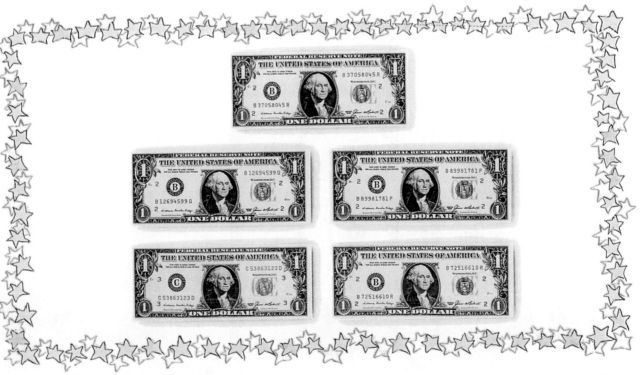

STUPENDOUS!
YOU'VE MADE TEN DOLLARS.

How would you like to be paid? One ten-dollar bill? Two five-dollar bills? Ten one-dollar bills? Or perhaps one five and five ones? Take your pick—they're all worth ten dollars.

or

or

If you prefer coins, you can have a five-foot stack of pennies (that's one thousand of them) or a fifteen-inch stack of two hundred nickels. You could also be paid with one hundred dimes, which would stack up to just over five inches. Or you can receive your ten dollars as a 3¼-inch pile of forty quarters.

You could spend your ten dollars on ten kittens or one thousand kitty snacks.

Or you could take your mom to the movies.

But maybe you'd rather save your money. If you leave your ten dollars in the bank for ten years, it will earn $6.40 in interest, and you will have $16.40.

If you leave it there for fifty years, your ten dollars will grow to $138.02.

YOU'VE WORKED HARD TO EARN
ONE HUNDRED DOLLARS.

You've decided to spend it on a plane ticket to the beach.
You could pay with a hundred-dollar bill, or two fifty-
dollar bills, or five twenty-dollar bills, or many other
combinations—six fives, three tens, and two twenties,
for instance.

Paying with pennies? You'll need ten thousand of them,
and they'll make a fifty-foot stack.

YOU'VE WORKED LONG AND HARD, AND YOU'VE EARNED A THOUSAND DOLLARS!

You're going to buy a pet. You could pay with coins or bills.

If you don't like the idea of carrying a thousand dollars around with you, you can put it in the bank and pay for the hippo with a check.

The check tells your bank to give $1,000 to the person who sold you the hippo.

GRACE
CHEERFUL AND WILLING INC.
Somewhere, U.S.A.

Pay to the order of _MR. HORACE HUGGABLE_ $ _1,000._ 00

ONE THOUSAND and 0/100 Dollars

Grace

THE BANK
Somewhere, U.S.A.

Here's how it works: You give the check to the person who sold you the hippo, and he gives it to his bank, and his bank sends it to a very busy clearinghouse in the city, and the clearinghouse tells your bank to take $1,000 out of your money.

After your bank does that, the clearinghouse tells the hippo salesman's bank to add $1,000 to his money, so he can take it and use it whenever, and however, he likes. Maybe he'll use it to raise more hippos.

If you used pennies to purchase a $10,000 Ferris wheel, someone might not be too happy about it. Even if you used ten thousand one-dollar bills, they would be mighty hard to handle.

Probably a check would be best.

MAGNIFICENT!

YOU'VE EARNED $50,000. And you've just read about a
well-worn, unloved, but perfectly fixable castle for sale.
The price: $100,000.

The castle costs $100,000 and you have only $50,000.
You're $50,000 short, but you can still buy the castle.
You could use the money you earned as a down payment
and ask a bank to lend you the rest.

Then you would pay the bank back, a little at a time, month after month . . . for many years.

But the amount you must pay the bank will be *more* than what you borrowed. That's because the bank charges for lending you money. The extra money is called interest, just like the interest the bank pays to you when it uses your money. Now you are using the bank's money, so you must pay interest to the bank.

If you have some very expensive plans, you may have to take on a tough job that pays well.

If you think ogre-taming would be an exciting challenge, you can have fun and make a great deal of money, too. Of course, you may not enjoy taming obstreperous ogres or building bulky bridges or painting purple pots. Enjoying your work is more important than money, so you should look for another job or make less expensive plans.

CONGRATULATIONS!
YOU'VE MADE A MILLION.

A MILLION DOLLARS!

That's a stack of pennies ninety-five miles high, or enough nickels to fill a school bus, or a whale's weight in quarters.

Would you prefer your million in paper money? Even a paper million is a hefty load: A million one-dollar bills would weigh 2,500 pounds and stack up to 360 feet.

What's the smallest your million could be? One-hundred-dollar bills are the largest made today, and it would take ten thousand of them to pay you for your feat of ogre-taming.

But a check for $1,000,000 would easily fit in your pocket or purse. And it's worth the same as the towering stacks of pennies or bills.

Now you can afford to buy tickets to the moon.

Or you can purchase some real estate for the endangered rhinoceroses.

But if you'd rather save your million than spend it, you could put it in the bank, where it would earn interest. The interest on a million is about $1,000 a week, or $143 a day, or $6 an hour, or 10 cents a minute. Just from sitting in the bank!

If you keep your million, you can probably live on the interest without doing any more work for the rest of your life. You might like that, or you could find it rather dull.

Making money means
making **choices**.

SO WHAT WOULD YOU DO IF YOU MADE A MILLION?

THINK AND RESPOND

1 What are some reasons people might have for doing business with a bank?

2 Where do you find out what jobs were done to earn the different amounts of money?

3 What does the author mean when he writes that making money means making **choices**?

4 What is the most interesting fact you learned from the article? How might you use this fact in the future?

5 How did you use reading strategies as you read this article? Give an example.

Imagine you wanted to write or illustrate a book that would be sold in bookstores. You would probably need an editor. An editor makes sure that a book is ready to be published. Here are some letters that David Schwartz and Steven Kellogg might have written to their editor.

From the Desk of
David M. Schwartz, Author

Dear Editor:

My earlier book, *How Much Is a Million?*, is about large numbers. I have always liked thinking about large numbers. Sometimes I wonder if anyone could ever count all the stars in the sky. Some of my readers have told me they like to think about large numbers too, especially numbers like a million dollars!

This gave me an idea for a new book. A book for children about money would be great. After all, they will be earning, spending, and saving money all their lives.

I will send you a draft of what I have in mind for the new book. Please contact Mr. Steven Kellogg, and tell him about this project. I would love to have him illustrate this book.

Sincerely,

David M. Schwartz

David M. Schwartz

FROM THE DESK OF

Steven Kellogg, Illustrator

Dear Editor:

Thank you for writing to me about the new project. I am very interested in working on Mr. Schwartz's new book, *If You Had a Million*. I am already thinking about the illustrations.

I think it is a wonderful idea to make a book that will help children understand money. The book would be even better if it were more about *earning* money. We could change the title to *If You Made a Million*. I think it is important that people earn money by doing work they enjoy. Maybe this book will show children that they can help others, earn money, and have fun, all at the same time!

I will send you some sketches soon. I look forward to working with you and Mr. Schwartz again.

Sincerely,

Steven Kellogg

Steven Kellogg

Visit *The Learning Site!*
www.harcourtschool.com

291

Suppose you have made some money by doing a job. You might decide to spend the money. You might look at advertisements like the one below to help you decide what to buy. Look at the example on these pages to learn about some of the parts of an advertisement.

STUPENDOUS STICKER STORE

"We Stick with You!"

A slogan, or catchy phrase

Is your sticker collection too small? Would you like to have the biggest collection of all your friends?

Come to the Stupendous Sticker Store.

A fact that can be proved

We've been selling stickers for more than twenty years, and *we have thousands of stickers to choose from!*

An opinion that cannot be proved

At the Stupendous Sticker Store, we believe that *the biggest collection is the best collection.*

Let us help you make your collection as big as it can be!

Don't Just Take Our Word for It!

Listen to what **Stevie "Wheels" Smith**, famous skateboarding champ, says about Stupendous Stickers!

An endorsement, or statement of approval given by a famous person.

"Stupendous Stickers are the best!"

Meet Stevie "Wheels" Smith in person at the Stupendous Sticker Store on Saturday at 10 A.M.!

Think and Respond
What decisions do you have to make when reading an advertisement?

293

Making Connections

Compare Texts

1 What did you learn from "If You Made a Million" about how people in communities earn money?

2 Why do the author and illustrator use a mixture of fantasy and fact in the text and art?

3 How is the author's purpose for writing "If You Made a Million" different from the author's purpose for writing the advertisement for the Stupendous Sticker Store?

4 How is "If You Made a Million" different from an encyclopedia article on the subject of money?

5 If you could speak to the author of "If You Made a Million," what other questions would you ask him about this topic?

Write a Page for a Travel Guide

A travel guide gives information about subjects such as weather, transportation, and money. Think about what a visitor from another country would need to know about American bills and coins. Write to inform travelers about American money. Use a graphic organizer like this one to plan your money page for a travel guide to the United States.

Writing CONNECTION

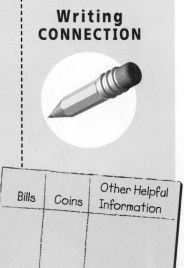

Bills	Coins	Other Helpful Information

Draw a Diagram

Look at the picture on page 287. Have you ever seen a real hot-air balloon? Research hot-air balloons to find out what happens to make them rise and then come back down. You may find information in an encyclopedia, in a nonfiction book, or at a science website for children. Draw a diagram to show how a hot-air balloon rises and comes down. Add labels and captions to help viewers understand what your diagram shows.

Science CONNECTION

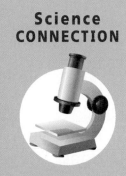

Compare Prices

"If You Made a Million" tells you that making money means making choices. This is because sometimes the same item costs more in one store than in another. Look through old newspapers and advertising flyers from stores. Find some advertisements for similar items. Cut out the ads and paste them on a sheet of paper. Circle one of the items or draw an arrow to show which one you would buy. Write a paragraph to explain your decision.

Math CONNECTION

295

Main Idea and Details

The **main idea** of a paragraph may be stated in one of its sentences. Often the first sentence tells what the paragraph is mostly about. Sometimes the last sentence does. The rest of the sentences give **supporting details** that tell more information about the main idea.

Sometimes the main idea of a paragraph or passage is not stated. You need to add up the details the author gives and state the main idea in your own words.

detail + detail + detail = main idea

The following sentences give details, but the main idea is not stated. How would you state the main idea of this paragraph?

You've decided to spend one hundred dollars on a plane ticket. You could pay with a hundred-dollar bill or two fifty-dollar bills or five twenty-dollar bills. You could even pay with ten ten-dollar bills or one hundred one-dollar bills.

Test Prep
Main Idea and Details

Spending Money

Everyone needs to learn how to spend money wisely. Once you spend your money, it's gone. Too often, we buy things and are sorry later. Nobody is happy when that happens.

Earning Money

You might earn money by weeding a garden. You might feed a cat when its owner is away. Some children earn money by running errands for older people in their neighborhood.

Now answer number 1. Base your answer on "Spending Money."

1. **Where is the main idea stated in the paragraph?**

   A The main idea is stated in the first sentence.

   B The main idea is stated in the second sentence.

   C The main idea is stated in the last sentence.

   D The main idea is not stated.

Tip

Remember that the main idea tells the most important idea, or what the paragraph is mostly about.

Now answer Number 2. Base your answer on "Earning Money."

2. **Write a sentence that tells the main idea of "Earning Money."**

Tip

Identify a topic that all the sentences give information about. That topic is the main idea.

Celebrate Our World

CONTENTS

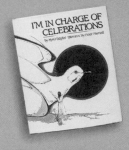

▲ I'm in Charge
  of Celebrations

average

celebrations

choosy

tracks

signal

admiring

Vocabulary Power

Do you enjoy the outdoors? The author of "I'm in Charge of Celebrations" loves nature and her home in the desert. People who live in other places also love their homes and the plants and creatures that live near them.

These pinecones may look **average**, but when they are painted and trimmed with ribbons, they will not be ordinary pinecones! They will brighten the house for holiday **celebrations**. We often include things from nature in our joyous events.

Winters in the north are cold and snowy. In the wild, animals can't be too **choosy** about their food. They must eat whatever they can find. We leave birdseed outside for the birds. Look at the **tracks** in the snow. It looks as if a squirrel has found the birdseed, too!

We enjoy this little plant that blooms to **signal** the end of winter. Its cheerful flowers announce the arrival of spring. Here is my mother **admiring** them. They are her favorite flowers, and she loves to look at them.

Vocabulary–Writing CONNECTION

What clues might tell you whether the season has changed? Write a paragraph that describes one or two things that **signal** the beginning of each new season.

301

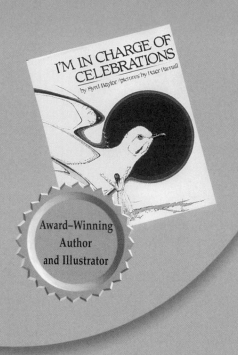

I'M IN CHARGE OF CELEBRATIONS
by Byrd Baylor/pictures by Peter Parnall

Award-Winning
Author
and Illustrator

Poem

A poem uses imagery, figurative language, and imagination to express feelings and ideas.

In this selection, look for

- the author's use of imagery.

- how the author creates rhythmical effects and some rhyme.

I'm in Charge of Celebrations

by *Byrd Baylor*

pictures by *Peter Parnall*

Sometimes
    people ask me,
     "Aren't you lonely
    out there
    with just
    desert
    around you?"

I guess they mean
the beargrass
and the yuccas
and the cactus
and the rocks.

I guess they mean
the deep ravines
and the hawk nests
in the cliffs
and the coyote trails
that wind
across the hills.

"Lonely?"

I can't help
laughing
when they ask me
that.

I always look at them . . .
surprised.

And I say,
"How could I be lonely?
I'm the one
in charge of
celebrations."

Sometimes
they don't believe me,
but it's true.
I am.

I put
myself
in charge.
I choose
my own.

Last year
I gave myself
one hundred and eight
celebrations—
besides the ones
that they close school for.

I cannot get by
with only
a few.

Friend, I'll tell you
how it works.

I keep a notebook
and I write the date
and then I write about
the celebration.

I'm very choosy
over
what goes in
that book.

It has to be something
I plan to remember
the rest of my life.

You can tell
what's worth
a celebration
because
your heart will
POUND
and
you'll feel
like you're standing
on top of a mountain
and you'll
catch your breath
like you were
breathing
some new kind of air.

Otherwise,
I count it just
an average day.
(I told you
I was
choosy.)

Friend, I wish you'd been here
for Dust Devil Day.

But since you weren't,
I'll tell you how
it got to be
my first
real
celebration.

You can call them
whirlwinds
if you want to.
Me, I think
dust devils
has a better sound.

Well, anyway,
I always stop
to watch them.
Here, everyone does.

You know how
they come
from far away,
moving
up from the flats,
swirling
and swaying
and falling

and turning,
picking up sticks
and sand
and feathers
and dry tumbleweeds.

Well, last March eleventh
we were all going somewhere.
I was in the back
of a pickup truck
when the dust devils
started
to gather.

You could see
they were
giants.

You'd swear
they were
calling
their friends
to come too.

And they came—
dancing
in time to
their own
windy music.

We all started counting.
We all started looking
for more.

They stopped that truck
and we turned
around
and around
watching them all.
There were seven.

At a time like that,
something
goes kind of crazy
in you.
You have to run
to meet them,
yelling
all the way.

You have to
whirl around
like you were
one of them,
and you can't stop
until
you're falling down.

And then all day
you think
how
lucky
you were
to be there.

Some of my best
celebrations
are sudden surprises
like that.

If you weren't outside
at that
exact
moment,
you'd miss them.

I spend a lot of time
outside
myself,
looking around.

Once
I saw a triple rainbow
that ended in a canyon
where I'd been
the day before.

I was halfway up a hill
standing
in a drizzle of rain.

It was almost dark
but I wouldn't go in
(because of the rainbows,
of course),
and there
at the top of the hill
a jackrabbit
was standing
up on his hind legs,
perfectly still,
looking straight
at that same
triple
rainbow.

I may be
the only person in the world
who's seen
a rabbit
standing in the mist
quietly watching
three rainbows.

That's worth
a celebration
any time.

I wrote it down
and drew the hill
and the rabbit
and the rainbow
and me.

Now
August ninth
is Rainbow Celebration Day.

308

I have
Green Cloud Day
too.

Ask anybody
and they'll tell you
clouds
aren't
green.

But
late one winter afternoon
I saw
this huge
green cloud.

It was not
bluish-green
or grayish-green
or something else.
This cloud
was
green . . .

green as a jungle parrot.

And the strange thing was
that it began
to take a parrot's shape,
first
the wings,
and then the head
and beak.

High in the winter sky
that green bird
flew.

It didn't last
more than a minute.
You know how fast
a cloud
can change,
but I still
remember
how it looked.

So I celebrate
green clouds
on February sixth.

At times like that,
I always think,
"What if I'd missed it?
What if I'd been
in the house?
Or what if I hadn't
looked up
when I did?"

You can see I'm
very lucky
about things
like that.

And
I was lucky
on Coyote Day,
because
out of all time
it had to be
one moment
only
that
a certain coyote
and I
could meet —
and we did.

Friend, you should have
been here too.

I was following
deer tracks,
taking my time,
bending down
as I walked,
kind of humming.
(I hum a lot
when I'm alone.)

I looked up
in time to see
a young coyote
trotting
through the brush.

She crossed
in front of me.
It was a windy day
and she was going east.

In that easy
silent way
coyotes move,
she pushed
into the wind.

I stood there
hardly breathing,
wishing I
could move
that way.

I was surprised
to see her
stop
and turn
and look
at me.

She seemed to think
that I was
just
another
creature
following another
rocky trail.

(That's true, of course.
I am.)

She didn't hurry.
She wasn't afraid.

I saw her eyes
and she saw
mine.

That look
held us
together.

Because of that,
I never will
feel
quite the same
again.

311

So
on September twenty-eighth
I celebrate
Coyote Day.

Here's what I do:
I walk
the trail
I walked that day,
and I hum
softly
as I go.

Finally,
I unwrap
the feast
I've brought for her.

Last time
it was three apples
and some pumpkin seeds
and an ear of corn
and some big soft homemade
ginger cookies.

The next day,
I happened to pass
that way again.
Coyote tracks
went all around
the rock
where the food had been,
and the food
was gone.

Next year
I'll make it even better.
I'll bring
an extra feast
and eat there too.

Another one
of my greatest
of all celebrations
is called
The Time of Falling Stars.

It lasts
almost a week
in the middle
of August,
and I wait
all year
for those hot
summer nights
when the sky
goes
wild.

You can call them
meteor showers
if you want to.
Me, I like to say
they're
falling stars.

All that week
I sleep outside.

I give
my full attention
to the sky.

And every time
a streak of light
goes
shooting
through the darkness,
I feel my heart
shoot
out of me.

One night
I saw
a fireball
that left
a long
red
blazing
trail
across the sky.

After it was
gone,
I stood there
looking up,
not quite
believing
what I'd seen.

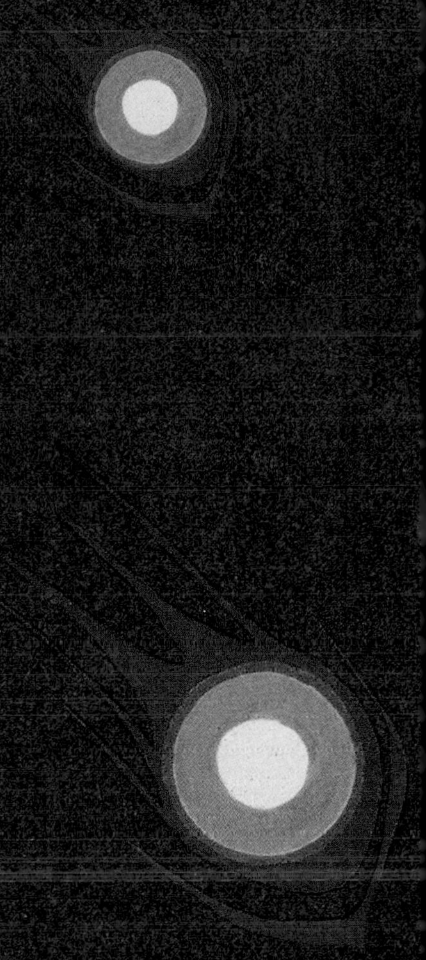

The strange thing was,
I met a man
who told me
he had seen it too
while he was lying
by a campfire
five hundred miles
away.

He said he did not sleep
again
that night.

Suddenly
it seemed
that we two
spoke a language
no one else
could
understand.

Every August
of my life,
I'll think of that.

Friend,
I've saved
my New Year Celebration
until last.

Mine
is a little
different
from the one
most people have.

It comes in
spring.

To tell the truth,
I never did
feel like
my new year
started
January first.

To me,
that's just
another
winter day.

I let my year
begin
when winter
ends
and morning light
comes
earlier,
the way it *should*.

That's when
I feel like
starting
new.

I wait
until
the white-winged doves
are back from Mexico,
and wildflowers
cover the hills,
and my favorite
cactus
blooms.

It always
makes me think
I ought to bloom
myself.

And
that's when
I start to plan
my New Year
Celebration.

I finally choose
a day
that is
exactly
right.

Even the air
has to be
perfect,
and the dirt
has to feel
good and warm
on bare feet.

(Usually,
it's a Saturday
around the end
of April.)

I have a drum
that I beat
to signal
The Day.

Then I go
wandering off,
following all
of my favorite
trails
to all of the
places
I like.

I check how
everything
is doing.

316

I spend the day
admiring
things.

If the old desert tortoise
I know from last year
is out
strolling around,
I'll go his direction
awhile.

I celebrate
with horned toads
and ravens
and lizards
and quail. . . .

And, Friend,
it's not
a bad
party.

Walking back home
(kind of humming),
sometimes
I think about
those people
who ask me if
I'm *lonely* here.

I have to
laugh
out
loud.

Think and Respond

1. Why does the narrator choose her own **celebrations?** How will she remember them all?

2. Why does the narrator laugh out loud when people ask if she is lonely?

3. Why does the narrator have her New Year Celebration in April instead of January?

4. Which of the celebrations in the poem is your favorite? Why do you like it?

5. Describe a reading strategy that helped you understand or enjoy the poem.

Meet the Author
Byrd Baylor

Dear Friends,

I'm in Charge of Celebrations is about my life and my home. I was born in Texas, and I spent many summers on a West Texas ranch. I love living where I can see cactus and red cliffs. I love hearing coyotes on cold, clear nights. These are the things I celebrate.

You can celebrate nature, too. Listen to the birds, and look at the flowers and the stones. Feel the wind and the sun and the rain. There are so many reasons to celebrate!

Yours truly,

Byrd Baylor

Meet the Illustrator
Peter Parnall

Dear Readers,

I love to study nature, especially animals. I almost became a veterinarian, but I decided I liked drawing animals more than doctoring them. I have been very happy drawing pictures for other authors' books. I have also written and illustrated some of my own books.

I now live and work on a farm in Maine. I enjoy taking long walks in the woods near the farm and sharing my art with children. I hope you enjoyed my pictures in *I'm in Charge of Celebrations*.

Yours truly,

Making Connections

Compare Texts

1 How does the author of "I'm in Charge of Celebrations" show her feelings about nature?

2 Why does the girl feel a close connection to the man who was five hundred miles away from her when he saw the fireball?

3 How is the girl's New Year celebration different from the other celebrations in the poem?

4 Think of another poem you have read. How is that poem like and unlike "I'm in Charge of Celebrations"?

5 What questions do you have about the desert as a result of reading "I'm in Charge of Celebrations"?

Write a Conversation

Writing CONNECTION

The girl in "I'm in Charge of Celebrations" tells about meeting a man who had also seen the fireball in the sky. Think about what these two people might have said to each other about the fireball. Write a conversation to express their thoughts and feelings. Use a graphic organizer like this one to plan your written conversation.

GIRL: _____

MAN: _____

GIRL: _____

MAN: _____

GIRL: _____

Experiment with Mirrors

The girl in the poem celebrates the day she saw a triple rainbow. Rainbows can occur when sunlight hits rain or mist. The light is bent at different angles by the drops of water and then is reflected out of the drops. Try to make a rainbow with mirrors or other shiny objects. Then look in a science book to find out why you did or did not succeed.

Science CONNECTION

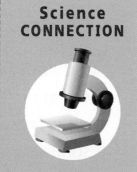

Draw a Map

"I'm in Charge of Celebrations" tells about life in a desert. Do research to learn about the desert that is closest to you, whether it is nearby or far away. Draw a map that shows where the desert is and also shows where your town or city is. Label the desert, your state, your town or city, and other states that may also be shown on your map. Identify and label other important features in your local region, such as lakes, rivers, oceans, mountains, or valleys.

Social Studies CONNECTION

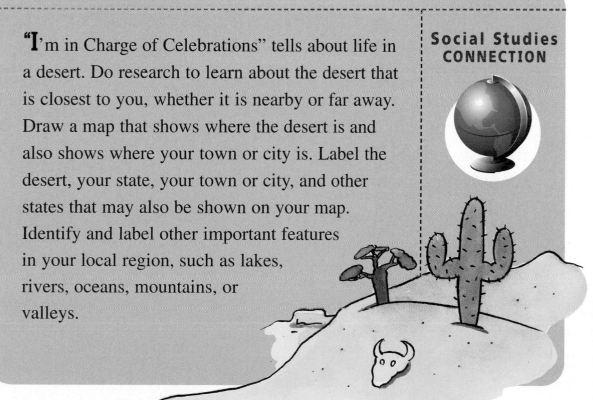

Summarize

You know that to make a good summary, you tell the most important ideas or events from a story in your own words. There is also another way to think about a summary. Only main ideas are included. Supporting details are not included.

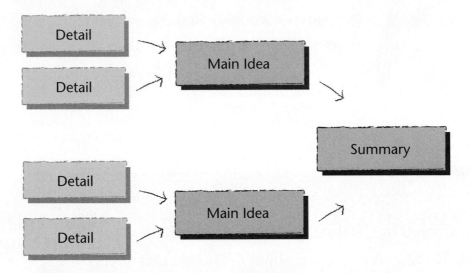

Think about the main ideas you would include in a summary of "I'm in Charge of Celebrations." Which of these statements belongs in a summary? Which are supporting details?

- A girl lives in the desert.

- She has long, dark hair.

- The girl once saw a rabbit watching a triple rainbow.

Test Prep
Summarize

▶ **Read the paragraph.**

The Cactus

Most types of cactus plants are well suited to the hot, dry climate of the desert. Their stems are large and can hold a lot of water. Many stems have special shapes that cause rain to run directly to the roots. The roots are near the surface and spread out over a wide area so they can take in any rain that falls. The plants usually grow far apart from each other so that each one has a large area of soil from which to soak up water.

Now answer Numbers 1 and 2. Base your answers on "The Cactus."

1. **Which of the following ideas belongs in a summary of the paragraph?**

   A   how much water a cactus can hold

   B   which parts of a cactus help it survive in the desert

   C   what cactus stems look like

   D   whether you have ever seen a cactus

Tip

Rule out the choices that give supporting details.

2. **Write a sentence that summarizes the paragraph.**

Tip

Remember that a good summary tells about the main ideas from the paragraph.

▲ Alejandro's Gift

growth

furrows

shunned

ample

windmill

cherished

Vocabulary Power

In the next selection, you will read about Alejandro. He grows many kinds of vegetables in his garden. It takes hard work to grow crops, whether in a small garden or on a large farm.

FARMING

Before farmers can plant crops, they must prepare the soil. First, they clear away any weeds, bushes, and other plant **growth**. Then they plow the soil to loosen it. The farmer in this tractor is using a plow to make long, deep grooves called **furrows**. He will plant the seeds for his crop in the furrows. Then he will cover the seeds with soil.

Farmers may spray or dust their crops with insect poisons. In recent years, some have **shunned** these sprays. They stay away from anything that may harm birds and other wildlife.

Crops can't grow without water. When there is **ample** rainfall, there is more than enough water to meet farmers' needs. When there is little rain, farmers need to get water in other ways. This **windmill** pumps water from the ground. It gets its power from the wind.

A farmer who has **cherished** his crop will usually have a good harvest. He will have worked hard because he cares deeply about the crop.

Vocabulary–Writing CONNECTION

What kinds of things have people **cherished** over the years? Write a paragraph that describes these things. Tell why you think people care about them.

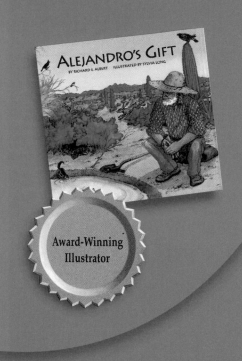

Award-Winning Illustrator

Genre

Realistic Fiction

Realistic fiction tells about characters and events that are like people and events in real life.

In this selection, look for

- **a main character who solves a problem.**
- **descriptive language that helps readers picture the setting.**

BY RICHARD E. ALBERT
ILLUSTRATED BY SYLVIA LONG

ALEJANDRO'S GIFT

Alejandro's small adobe house stood beside a lonely desert road.

Beside the house stood a well, and a windmill to pump water from the well. Water for Alejandro and for his only companion, a burro.

It was a lonely place, and Alejandro welcomed any who stopped by to refresh themselves at the well. But visitors were few, and after they left, Alejandro felt lonelier than before.

To more easily endure the lonely hours, Alejandro planted a garden. A garden filled with carrots, beans, and large brown onions.

Tomatoes and corn.

Melons, squash, and small red peppers.

Most mornings found Alejandro tending the garden, watching it grow. These were times he cherished, and he often stayed for hours, working until driven indoors by the desert heat.

The days went by, one after another with little change, until one morning when there was an unexpected visitor. This visitor came not from the desert road, but from the desert itself.

A ground squirrel crept from the underbrush. Moving
warily over the sand, it hesitated and looked around. Alejandro
paused, keeping very quiet as the squirrel approached the
garden. It ran up to one of the furrows, drank its fill of water,
and scampered away. After it left, Alejandro realized that for
those few moments his loneliness had been all but forgotten.

And because he felt less lonely, Alejandro found himself
hoping the squirrel would come again.

The squirrel did come again, from time to time bringing
along small friends.

Wood rats and pocket gophers.

Jackrabbits, kangaroo rats, pocket mice.

Birds, too, became aware of Alejandro's garden.

Roadrunners, gila woodpeckers, thrashers.

Cactus wrens, sage sparrows, mourning doves, and others came in the evening to perch on the branches of a mesquite bush, or to rest on the arms of a lone saguaro, before dropping down for a quick drink before nightfall.

Occasionally, even an old desert tortoise could be seen plodding toward the garden.

Suddenly, Alejandro found that time was passing more quickly. He was rarely lonely. He had only to look up from his hoe, or from wherever he might be at any moment, to find a small friend nearby.

For a while this was all that mattered to Alejandro, but after a time he wasn't so sure. He began asking himself if there was something more important than just making himself less lonely. It took Alejandro little time to see there was.

He began to realize that his
tiny desert friends came to his garden not
for company, but for water. And he found himself thinking
of the other animals in the desert.

Animals like the coyote and the desert gray fox.

The bobcats, the skunks, the badgers, the long-nosed coatis.

The peccaries, sometimes called *javelinas*, the short-
tempered wild pigs of the desert.

The antlered mule deer, the does, and the fawns.

Finding enough water was not a problem. With his windmill
and well, Alejandro could supply ample water for any and all.
Getting it to those who needed it was something else.

The something else, Alejandro decided, was a desert water hole.

Without delay, Alejandro started digging. It was tiring work, taking many days in the hot desert sun. But the thought of giving water to so many thirsty desert dwellers more than made up for the drudgery. And when it was filled, Alejandro was pleased with the gift he had made for his desert friends.

There was good reason to suppose it would take time for the larger animals to discover their new source of water, so

Alejandro was patient. He went about as usual, feeding his burro, tending the garden, and doing countless other chores.

Days passed and nothing happened. Still, Alejandro was confident. But the days turned to weeks, and it was still quiet at the water hole. Why, Alejandro wondered, weren't they coming? What could he have done wrong?

The absence of the desert folk might have remained a mystery had Alejandro not come out of the house one morning when a skunk was in the clearing beyond the water hole. Seeing Alejandro, the skunk darted to safety in the underbrush.

It suddenly became very clear why Alejandro's gift was being shunned.

Alejandro couldn't believe he had been so thoughtless, but what was important now was to put things right as quickly as possible.

Water hole number two was built far from the house and screened by heavy desert growth. When it was filled and ready, Alejandro waited with mixed emotions. He was hopeful, yet he couldn't forget what had happened the first time.

As it turned out, he was not disappointed.

The animals of the desert did come, each as it made its own discovery. Because the water hole was now sheltered from the small adobe house and the desert road, the animals were no longer fearful. And although Alejandro could not see through

the desert growth surrounding the water hole, he had ways of knowing it was no longer being shunned.

By the twitter of birds gathering in the dusk.

By the rustling of mesquite in the quiet desert evening telling of the approach of a coyote, a badger, or maybe a desert fox.

By the soft hoofbeats of a mule deer, or the unmistakable sound of a herd of peccaries charging toward the water hole.

And in these moments when Alejandro sat quietly
listening to the sounds of his desert neighbors, he knew that
the gift was not so much a gift that he had given, but a gift he
had received.

THINK AND RESPOND

1 What gift does Alejandro give, and what gift does he
receive?

2 What kind of person is Alejandro? How do you know?

3 Why is Alejandro's first water hole **shunned** by the
animals?

4 Would you enjoy a visit to Alejandro's home? Explain
your answer.

5 What strategies did you use to help you understand
"Alejandro's Gift"? When did you use them?

MEET THE AUTHOR
Richard E. Albert

Richard E. Albert spent most of his life working as an engineer for a gas company. He wrote some Western stories, as well as stories for children's magazines. Then, when he was eighty-three, he wrote *Alejandro's Gift*. It was the first book he had written for children.

MEET THE ILLUSTRATOR
Sylvia Long

Drawing and horses were always on Sylvia Long's mind when she was a child. Her favorite birthday presents were crayons, paints, and pencils. She also wished for a horse on every birthday. Finally she got her own horse after she was married.

Today Sylvia Long lives in Arizona and draws pictures for magazines and picture books. She says that she feels "so lucky to be able to draw and call it work."

Visit *The Learning Site!*
www.harcourtschool.com

Seeds Can Sleep
by Mary Brown

Each bump in the pod contains one fruit. A fruit is about the size and shape of a peanut, and it holds one seed.

Like animals, plants need water to live. Some plants have structures that let them live for a long time without water. The lotus is such a plant. Its seed can be kept dry for many years before it is germinated, or made to grow. In fact, one scientist in California germinated a seed that was more than 1,000 years old! This is the oldest seed ever reported to sprout.

In 1982, Dr. Jane Shen-Miller was given seven lotus fruits as a gift. The fruits had been found deep underground by scientists in Beijing, China. Because they were far beneath the earth, Dr. Shen-Miller knew that the fruits must have fallen a very long time ago.

342

So she and a team of scientists studied the seeds of the fruits to find out how old they were. The oldest seed was about 1,288 years old. The youngest was about 95 years old.

Next, Dr. Shen-Miller began the process of germination. She carefully cut a hole in the outer shell of the oldest seed. After a thousand-year sleep, the ancient seed was given air and water. It grew a little green shoot in only four days.

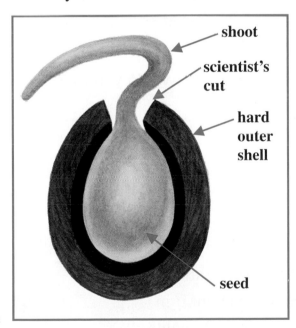

Cross-section of the lotus seed

How could a seed lie dormant, alive but not growing, for so many years? Research shows several reasons for the lotus seed's survival.

Most important was the hard shell of the seed. The shell protected the seed from changes in the weather and from harmful bacteria. Plus, the shell held in just the right amount of water for the seed. Another reason the seed could sprout after a thousand years is that it was somehow able to repair itself. Scientists are trying to find out how.

Research on this amazing plant continues today. Scientists hope that their research will help them find ways to protect and store useful crops, such as corn and wheat. If we find a way to keep crops alive longer, how will this affect the way we share food with the rest of the world?

The mature seed pod on the right shows how the fruit are exposed.

Think and Respond

Why is the lotus seed important to scientists?

Making Connections

Compare Texts

1 How is "Alejandro's Gift" related to the theme Celebrate Our World?

2 How do the birds and small animals in the story behave differently from the larger animals?

3 Why does the author of "Alejandro's Gift" use more colorful language than the author of "Seeds Can Sleep"?

4 What is another realistic fiction story you have read that tells about wildlife? Which story is better at showing how people should treat wild animals? Explain your answer.

5 Which of the animals in "Alejandro's Gift" would you most like to learn more about? Tell why.

Write a Journal Entry

The first day the animals start coming to the new water hole is special for Alejandro. Think about what Alejandro would say if he wrote about it in his journal. Write to express Alejandro's thoughts and feelings.

Use a graphic organizer like this one to plan Alejandro's journal entry.

Writing CONNECTION

When and where did the events take place?	What happened?	How do I (Alejandro) feel about it?

Investigate Windmills

Alejandro in "Alejandro's Gift" has a windmill for pumping water from his well. Windmills have been used for hundreds of years to pump water and grind grain. Do research to find out how a windmill uses wind energy to do work. Show the results of your research in a picture or diagram with labels and captions, or by constructing a model and explaining how it works.

Give an Oral Presentation

Alejandro planted a variety of vegetables in his desert garden. The kinds of plants that grow in a region depend on the soil and climate. How did Native Americans get food from the land long ago? What foods did they have? How did the climate and resources in the region affect the way they got their food? Research these questions, and prepare an oral presentation to share your information.

Cause and Effect

In stories, one event often leads to another. The reason an event happens is the **cause**. What happens is the **effect**. Here are some examples from "Alejandro's Gift."

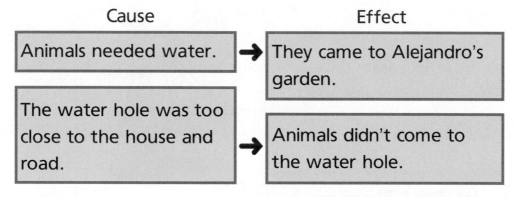

Cause | Effect

Cause		Effect
Animals needed water.	→	They came to Alejandro's garden.
The water hole was too close to the house and road.	→	Animals didn't come to the water hole.

Authors often use signal words for causes and effects.

And <u>because</u> he felt less lonely, Alejandro found himself hoping the squirrel would come again.

<u>Because</u> signals that the author is telling about a cause and effect. Other signal words and phrases include <u>so that</u>, <u>since</u>, <u>as a result</u>, <u>therefore</u>, <u>for this reason</u>, <u>in order to</u>, and <u>so</u>.

Often you will need to use your own knowledge to figure out causes and effects in stories. You can also ask yourself questions. To find an effect, ask "What happened?" To find a cause, ask "Why did it happen?"

Visit *The Learning Site!*
www.harcourtschool.com

See *Skills* and *Activities*

Test Prep
Cause and Effect

▶ **Read the paragraphs.**

> Betsy was lonely. She couldn't have a pet because pets were not allowed in her building. Then one day Betsy saw an advertisement in the newspaper. "If I had a bird feeder like the one in the ad," Betsy said, "then I wouldn't be lonely anymore."
>
> Betsy was right. Soon many birds began to come to her feeder. She loved to sit and watch them.

1. **What caused Betsy to be lonely?**

   A She lived in an apartment building.

   B She saw an advertisement in the newspaper.

   C She could not have a pet.

   D She wanted a bird feeder.

Tip

Use your own knowledge of causes and effects to choose the answer that makes sense.

2. **What was the effect of Betsy's seeing the advertisement?**

   F She could not have a pet.

   G She got a bird feeder.

   H She was lonely.

   J She lived in an apartment building.

Tip

Keep in mind that the effect happens after the cause.

Vocabulary Power

coast
edges
epicenter
range
magma
peak

The selection "Rocking and Rolling" tells about some of the mighty forces that shape Earth. Read this newspaper article about earthshaking events.

Quake shakes town

Yesterday's earthquake caused damage to this house.

A small earthquake was felt yesterday on the **coast**. People living in towns near the sea were surprised, but no one was hurt. The only damage reported was to the **edges** of a roof. An old tree fell against the corner of the house and broke tiles on two sides of the roof.

The **epicenter** of yesterday's earthquake is one hundred miles from here. This place on the earth's surface is just above the center of the earthquake. It is located in a mountain **range** that includes an active volcano.

Scientists think this earthquake may be a signal that the volcano will erupt soon. They believe that **magma**, or melted rock, is working its way upward from deep in the earth. This movement can cause small earthquakes. When it reaches the **peak**, or top, of the mountain, the volcano will erupt.

Scientists will watch closely to see what happens. They stated that they are sure no one is in any danger.

**Vocabulary–Writing
CONNECTION**

Would you like to live along a sea **coast** or near a mountain **range**? Write a paragraph that explains the reasons for your choice.

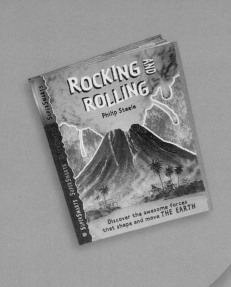

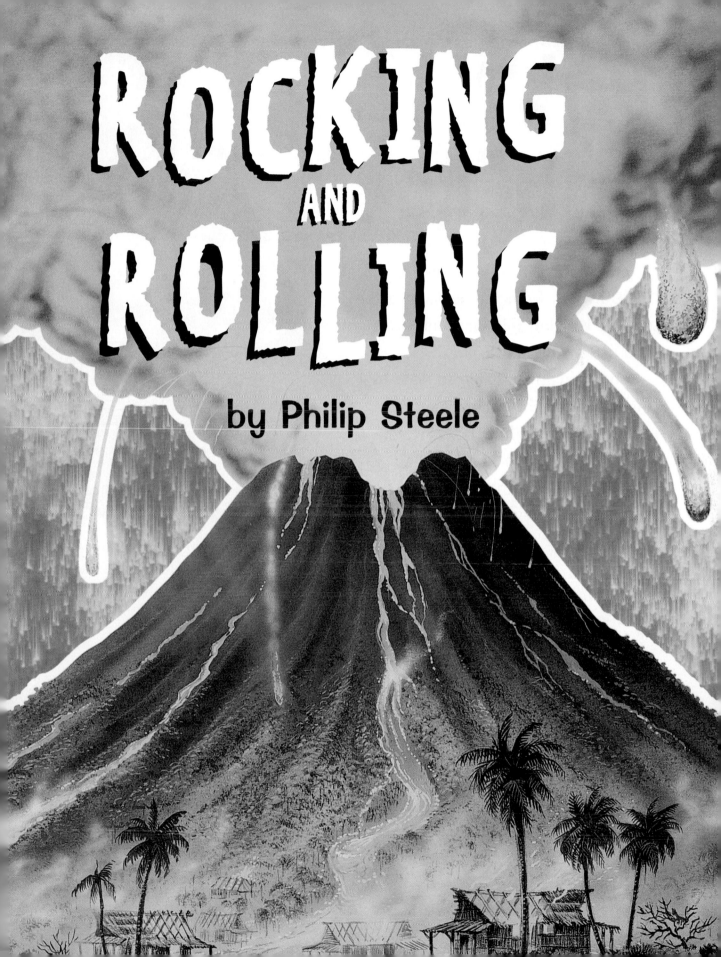

ROCKING
AND
ROLLING

by Philip Steele

DOWN UNDER

Our planet Earth is huge—about 3,960 miles from the surface to the center. Walking this far would take you about 55 days and nights.

You wouldn't be able to walk to the center of the earth, though, as it's incredibly hot. It's at least 9,000°F, which is nearly the same temperature as the surface of the sun.

Outer core

Inner core

Earth has four layers. The top one is called the crust and it's made of rock. It's about 25 miles thick under the land, but only about 5 miles thick beneath the ocean.

The mantle is next. It's also made of rock, but it's so hot that some parts have melted into magma and are as gooey as oatmeal.

Beneath the mantle is Earth's core. This is made of metal and has two layers—an outer and an inner core.

The outer core is runny because it's so hot. But although the inner core is even hotter, it's solid. Why? Because the other three layers are pressing down on it and the weight is enough to squash it solid!

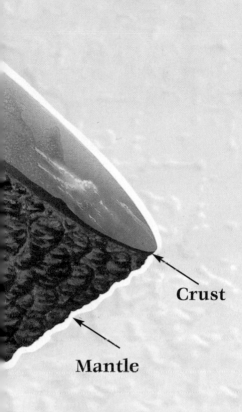

Crust

Mantle

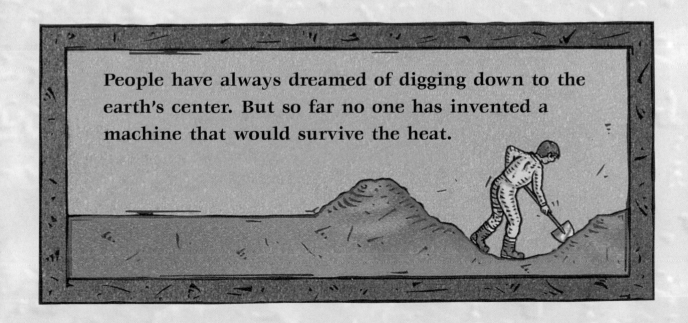

People have always dreamed of digging down to the earth's center. But so far no one has invented a machine that would survive the heat.

353

CRACKING UP

If all the oceans disappeared, Earth would look just like a jigsaw puzzle made up of lots of big pieces.

The pieces are called plates, and there are about 20 of them. They float on the lower part of the earth's mantle, moving very, very slowly—between 1 and 8 inches per year.

Sometimes the plates move apart and gooey magma rises up from the mantle to fill the gap. The magma cools and hardens to form new land or ocean floor.

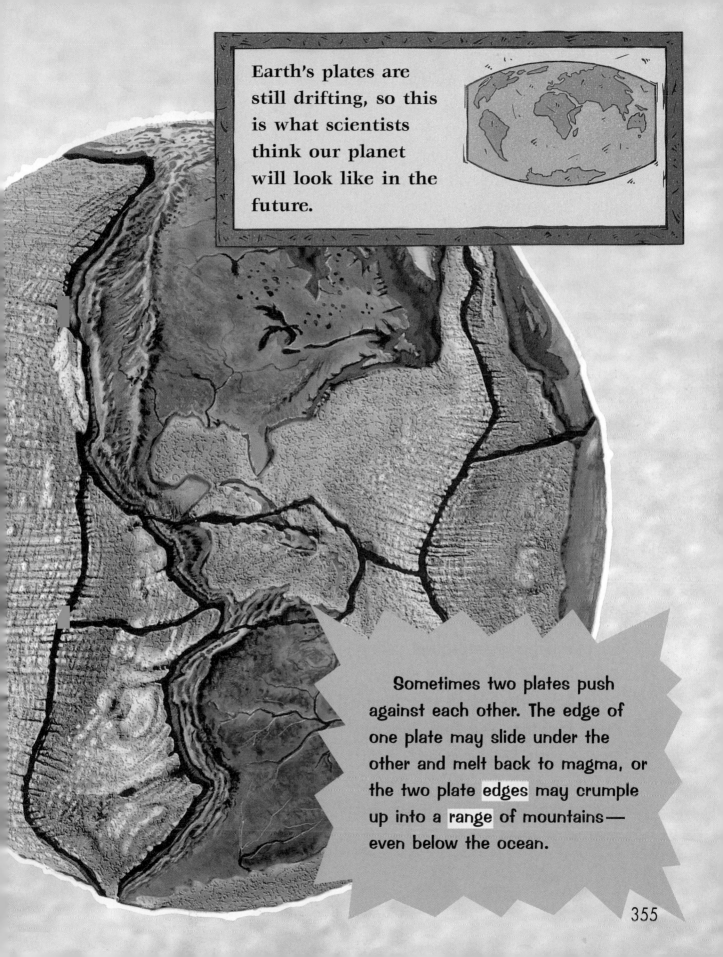

Earth's plates are still drifting, so this is what scientists think our planet will look like in the future.

Sometimes two plates push against each other. The edge of one plate may slide under the other and melt back to magma, or the two plate edges may crumple up into a range of mountains—even below the ocean.

QUAKE AND

Just a few minutes ago this truck was speeding along the road. Then, suddenly, there was a terrifying roar, and the ground opened up—an earthquake!

The most serious earthquakes happen deep underground, along the edges of the earth's plates.

Usually, the plates stay jammed close together. But from time to time a plate breaks away.

This makes the ground shudder and shake. Sometimes it can even split wide open.

SHAKE

These shudders can be felt thousands of miles away because they spread out from the earthquake's epicenter like the ripples from a stone thrown into a pond.

Every year, there are 40,000 to 50,000 earthquakes that are strong enough to be felt. However, only about 40 of them are big enough to cause any damage.

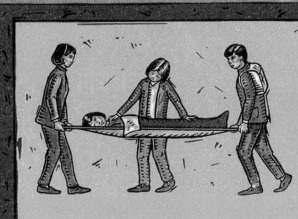

In Japan there's a National Disaster Prevention Day each year, when everyone practices what to do during an earthquake. Volunteers spend the day learning how to rescue people from fallen buildings.

WALLS OF

Most waves are made by the wind blowing over the sea. This is no ordinary wave, though. It's called a tsunami, and it was started by an earthquake.

A big earthquake is a lot like a huge bomb going off. The force of the explosion can create a tsunami that travels thousands of miles through the ocean.

When the tsunami is in deep ocean water, its top may be only 8–12 inches above the surface.

But as it rolls on into shallower water near the coast, the tsunami is forced upward into a gigantic wall of water— sometimes it can be even higher than an apartment building!

HIGHER AND HIGHER

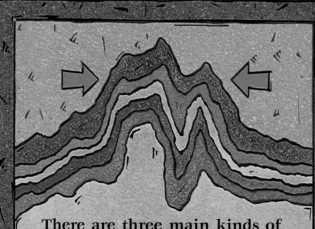

There are three main kinds of mountains. Fold mountains, like the Himalayas, form when the earth's plates crunch into one another, and layers of the crust are pushed up into loops and bumps.

Dome mountains happen when magma bulges up beneath the crust. This forces the crust up into a large rounded hump—much like the back of an elephant!

Block mountains are made when part of the crust is forced up between two cracks in a plate. These cracks are called faults.

Welcome to the top of the world. The Himalayas are the highest mountain ranges on Earth, and the tallest Himalayan peak is Mount Everest.

Everest already soars to a height of 29,029 feet. But next year it will be a tiny bit higher—it's still growing.

The Himalayas started forming around 53 million years ago when the earth's plate carrying the land that is now India began crunching upward into the rest of Asia.

Inch by inch, India pushed northward. And over tens of millions of years, the plate edges crumpled into the huge ridges, peaks, and valleys we see today.

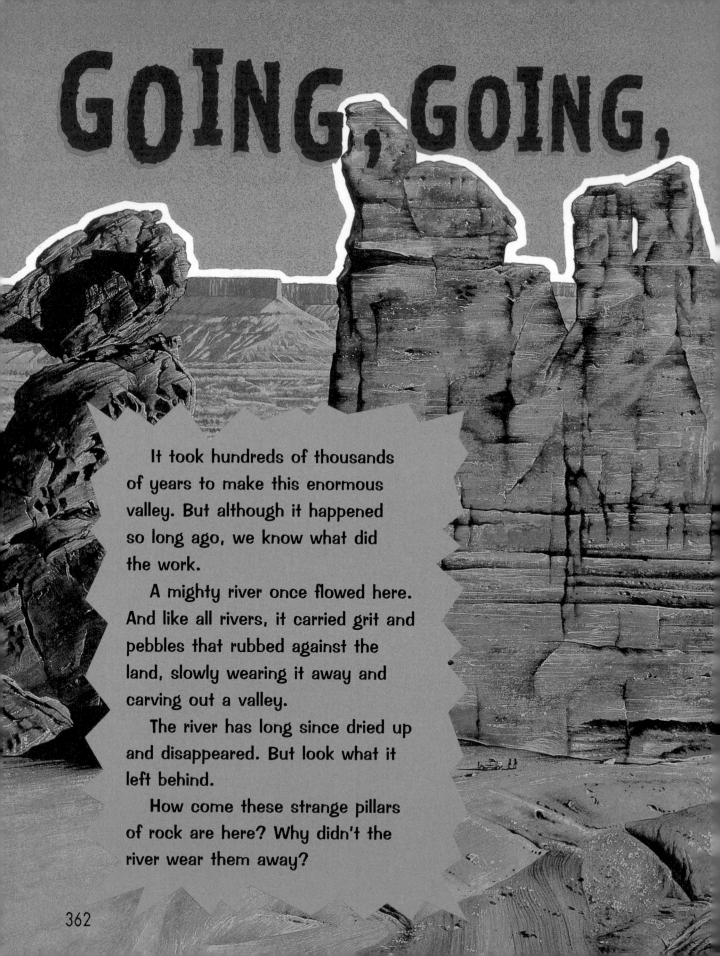

GOING, GOING,

It took hundreds of thousands of years to make this enormous valley. But although it happened so long ago, we know what did the work.

A mighty river once flowed here. And like all rivers, it carried grit and pebbles that rubbed against the land, slowly wearing it away and carving out a valley.

The river has long since dried up and disappeared. But look what it left behind.

How come these strange pillars of rock are here? Why didn't the river wear them away?

GONE!

Well, some rocks are harder than others, and hard rocks break down more slowly than soft ones. The river dried up before it had time to wear these pillars away.

The wearing away of the land is called erosion, and it's still going on today. But water isn't doing the work now—so what is?

The answer is blowing in the wind. Day after day it whistles through the valley, picking up grit and sand and blasting everything it touches.

The wind works like sandpaper, slowly wearing the rocks down and grinding them into weird and wonderful shapes.

Rock is much harder than wind and water—yet given time, wind and water are powerful enough to shape the land we live on.

Think and Respond

1. Will Earth look the same in one million years as it does now? How do you know?

2. Why is certain information placed in boxes or frames?

3. How does *magma* change the shape of Earth's surface?

4. What is one fact you learned from "Rocking and Rolling" that you did not know before?

5. How did using a reading strategy help you as you read this selection?

MEET THE AUTHOR PHILIP STEELE

Philip Steele would make an interesting employee. Look over this application. What information might tell you that he is a good writer? Would you hire him to write for you?

Application for Employment

Name **Philip Steele**	Job Desired **Author**

Address   Ynys Môn, Wales, United Kingdom

Education   University College, Durham

Work History
English teacher, Germany
Editor for educational books, London, England
Writer and editor, North Wales

Hobbies   **Traveling, backpacking**
Other Languages   **Welsh**

Special Skills and Interests
**I am curious and want to learn new things.
I enjoy history and nature. I also visit local
schools to keep in touch with children's interests.**

Published Works	**(Do you have another**
The Greek News	**sheet of paper so**
The Blue Whale	**that I can list all of**
The People Atlas	**them?)**

Visit *The Learning Site!*
www.harcourtschool.com

Making Connections

Compare Texts

1 How does "Rocking and Rolling" give readers a better understanding of our world?

2 Why does the author divide the text into sections?

3 Why do you think the author put the sections in the order that he did? Explain your answer.

4 Name another nonfiction selection you have read that also includes diagrams. Which did you find easier to understand, "Rocking and Rolling" or the other selection? Tell why.

5 What topic or topics that the author tells about in "Rocking and Rolling" would you be most interested in exploring further?

Write a News Story

Writing CONNECTION

In "Rocking and Rolling," you read about earthquakes and tsunamis. Think about what might happen during and after an earthquake or a tsunami and how a news reporter would write about it. Then write a news story to inform the newspaper readers.

Use a graphic organizer like this one to plan your news story. Make up realistic details based on information from "Rocking and Rolling."

What?	
When?	
Where?	
Who?	
Why?	

Write a Report

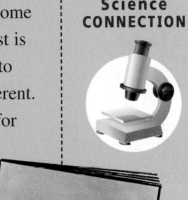

In "Rocking and Rolling," you learned that some rocks are harder than others. The Earth's crust is made up of three types of rock. Do research to find out what they are and how they are different.

Write a report with three sections, one for each type of rock. Be sure to write a heading for each section. Include illustrations and diagrams if you wish. You might also want to collect some rock samples and decide what types of rock they might be.

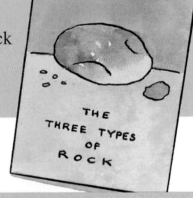

THE THREE TYPES OF ROCK

Estimate Distances

The distance from the surface of the Earth to its center is almost 4,000 miles. Suppose you traveled 4,000 miles north, south, east, or west from your home, on the Earth's surface. Look at a world map and estimate where you might be at the end of your journey. Then use the scale on the map to measure exactly where you would be.

Estimated Location from Home	Actual Location from Home

Locate Information

Focus Skill

Imagine how the selection "Rocking and Rolling" would look as a book. What parts might the nonfiction book have? How could you use these parts of the book to find information?

Part of Book	Description	Example
title	• the name of a book, unit, chapter, or story	**Rocking and Rolling**
table of contents	• a list of the titles with the page numbers • near the front of a book	**Table of Contents** Down Under 352 Cracking Up 354 Quake and Shake 356
chapter heading	• title at the beginning of each new chapter	**Down Under** (on page 352)
glossary	• dictionary of terms used in the book • in the back of the book	**Glossary** **range** [rānj] *n.* A row or line of mountains
index	• alphabetical list of topics and page numbers • in the back of a book	**Index** magma 353, 354, 360 mantle 353 mountains 360–361

Visit *The Learning Site!*
 www.harcourtschool.com

See *Skills* and *Activities*

Test Prep
Locate Information

▶ **Here is the table of contents for a book about volcanoes.**

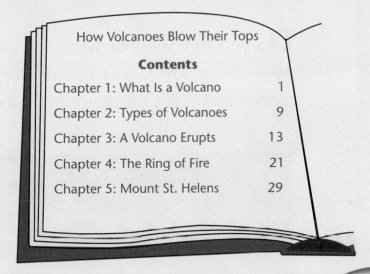

How Volcanoes Blow Their Tops

Contents

1. **"A Volcano Erupts" is—**

   A a book title

   B a chapter title

   C a story title

   D listed alphabetically

> **Tip**
> Look carefully at the information that the table of contents gives you.

2. **You could use this table of contents to find out—**

   F the meaning of the word *erupts*

   G which pages tell about lava

   H on what pages you can read about the Ring of Fire

   J why scientists study volcanoes

> **Tip**
> Look at the table of contents provided. Which of the answer choices matches a chapter title?

Vocabulary Power

eventually

universe

sphere

continent

converse

homeward

Do you ever wonder what lies beyond your own city or town, your country, or your own planet Earth? It's natural to be curious.

DANNY: Dad, will people ever travel to other planets?

DAD: Maybe they will **eventually**, but not very soon.

DANNY: How big is the **universe**, Dad?

DAD: It's too big to measure. The universe contains everything that exists—all the stars you see in the sky, the moon, the sun, the planets, and all of space.

DANNY: Wow, that's bigger than I thought! (*He is silent for a moment.*) Dad, why does the moon change its shape?

DAD: It doesn't really change shape. The moon is a **sphere**. It is round like a ball, but we see only part of it. The part we see changes as the moon moves around the earth.

DANNY: Dad, my teacher said we live on the **continent** of North America. She said a continent is a large area of land. How many continents are there?

DAD: There are seven continents, Danny. We can find them on our map of the world when we get home. We could **converse** about this for hours. I've enjoyed our talk. (*He looks at his watch.*) It's getting late. We'd better head **homeward**.

DANNY: Okay, I'm ready to start toward home now.

Vocabulary–Writing CONNECTION

A circle is a flat shape, but a **sphere** is round like a ball. Write a list of objects that are like spheres and a list of objects that are like circles.

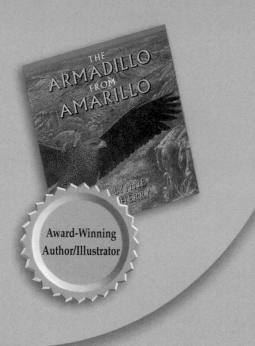

Award-Winning Author/Illustrator

Informational Narrative

An informational narrative is a story that presents information and facts.

In this selection, look for

- elements of fiction and nonfiction.

- information about a topic.

The from

TEXAS ARMADILLO
This burrowing mammal is covered with a bony shell. When attacked, the armadillo may roll up like a ball and depend upon its own armor for protection. Armadillos feed on fruits, roots, and insects.

Distributed by Austin News Agency, Austin Texas

SAN ANTONIO, TX
P.M
25 APR
1993

Dear Brillo,
I've lately had the urge to go and visit San Antonio, a city I've not seen before that my friends tell me I'd adore. ♡
Sasparillo

BLUEBONNETS
SAN ANTONIO
TEXAS

ADILLO

SAN ANTONIO
P.M.
MAY
1993

Dear Brillo,
Hi and warm regards from your cousin Sasparillo. I lay my head and slept today on a blue bluebonnet pillow.
Love,
Sasparillo

Armadillo Amarillo

written and illustrated by Lynne Cherry

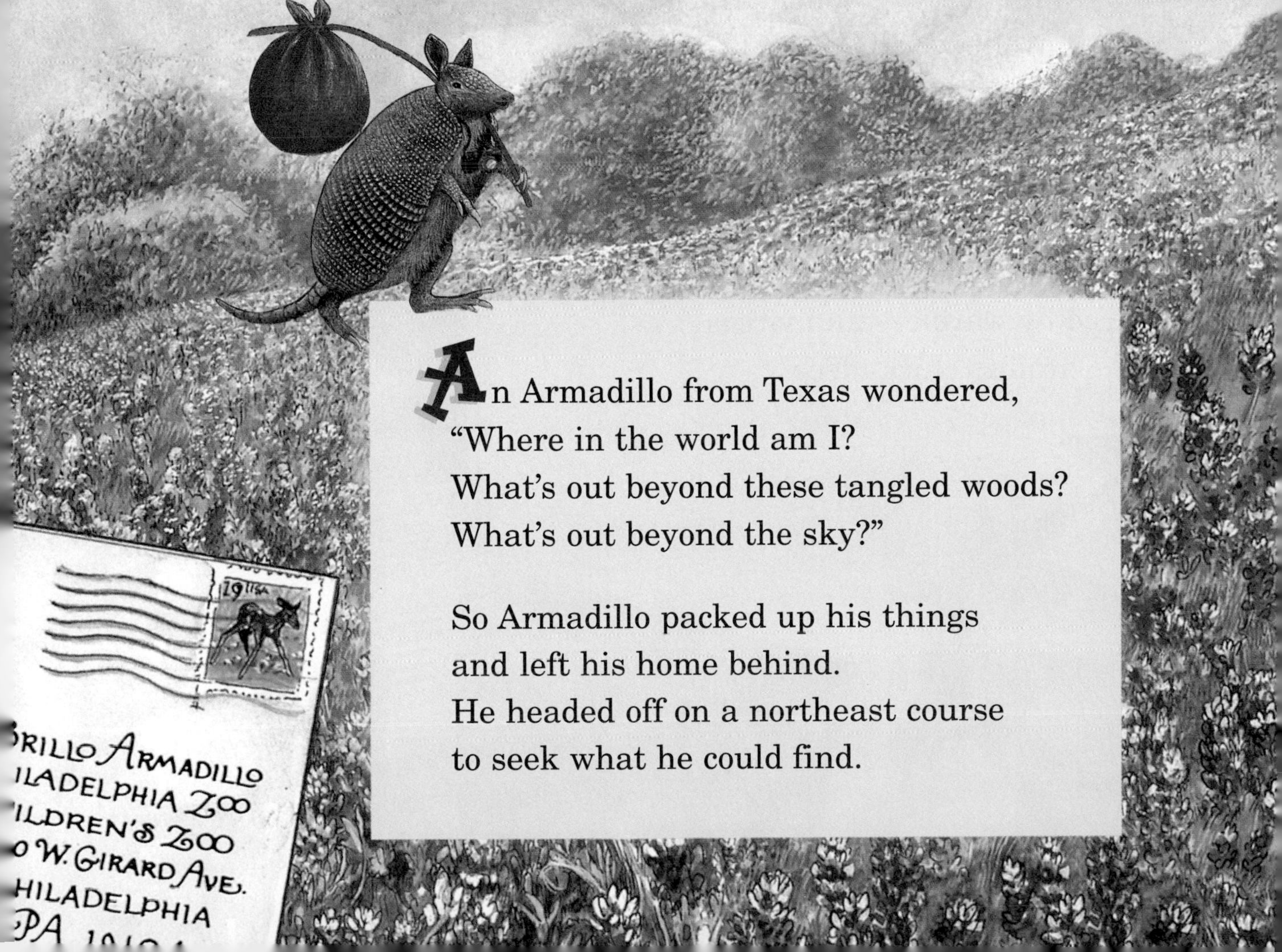

An Armadillo from Texas wondered,
"Where in the world am I?
What's out beyond these tangled woods?
What's out beyond the sky?"

So Armadillo packed up his things
and left his home behind.
He headed off on a northeast course
to seek what he could find.

ARMADILLO
ILADELPHIA ZOO
ILDREN'S ZOO
O W. GIRARD AVE.
HILADELPHIA
PA

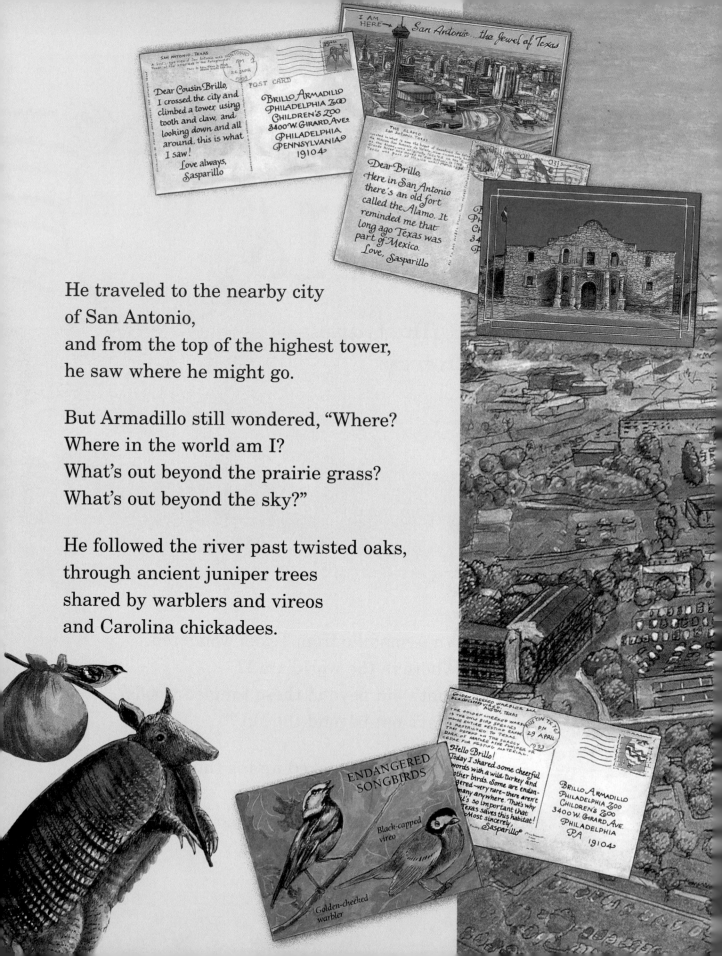

He traveled to the nearby city
of San Antonio,
and from the top of the highest tower,
he saw where he might go.

But Armadillo still wondered, "Where?
Where in the world am I?
What's out beyond the prairie grass?
What's out beyond the sky?"

He followed the river past twisted oaks,
through ancient juniper trees
shared by warblers and vireos
and Carolina chickadees.

Dear Cousin Brillo,
I crossed the city and
climbed a tower, using
tooth and claw, and
looking down and all
around, this is what
I saw!
    Love always,
    Sasparillo

POST CARD

BRILLO ARMADILLO
PHILADELPHIA ZOO
CHILDREN'S ZOO
3400 W. GIRARD AVE.
PHILADELPHIA
PENNSYLVANIA
19104

Dear Brillo,
Here in San Antonio
there's an old fort
called the Alamo. It
reminded me that
long ago Texas was
part of Mexico.
    Love, Sasparillo

ENDANGERED
SONGBIRDS

Black-capped
vireo

Golden-cheeked
warbler

Hello Brillo!
Today I shared some cheerful
words with a wild turkey and
other birds. Some are endangered—very rare—there aren't
many anywhere. That's why
it's so important that
Texas saves this habitat!
    Most sincerely,
    Sasparillo

BRILLO ARMADILLO
PHILADELPHIA ZOO
CHILDREN'S ZOO
3400 W. GIRARD AVE.
PHILADELPHIA
PA
19104

The landscape changed dramatically
through woodland, towns, and plains.
Armadillo explored canyons
and walked through heavy rains.

He walked for weeks and came to Austin,
continued west and north
to Abilene and Lubbock,
he hiked and sallied forth.

Armadillo often along the way
climbed up to higher ground.
He scurried up the canyon walls
and stopped to look around.

How different were the plains above—
flowers went on for a mile!
Armadillo decided to settle down
and stay there for a while.

ENCHANTED ROCK
AUSTIN, TEXAS

ENCHANTED ROCK
A sacred place of the
Indians.

Dear Brillo,
I much prefer the
night to traveling
during the day. So
sometimes I look for
a cranny or nook to
sleep the sun away.
Love, Sasparillo

POST CA

BRILLO ARM
PHILADELPHI
CHILDREN'S
3400 W. GIRARD
PHILADELPHIA, PA

Howdy from Texas!

Dear Brillo,
I'm near Amarillo.
This land is cool and
flat! It's definitely
an inadequate
Armadillo habitat!
I'll be the only
Armadillo who lives
near the city of
Amarillo!
♥ Sasparillo

POST CARD

BRILLO ARMADILLO
PHILADELPHIA ZOO
CHILDREN'S ZOO
3400 W. GIRARD AVE.
PHILADELPHIA, PA
19104

20 JUNE
1993

But Armadillo still wondered, "Where?
Where in the world *am* I?
Perhaps I'd have a better idea
if I could somehow fly."

One day he asked the golden eagle
as she came breezing by,
"What can I do for a bird's-eye view
from up in the big blue sky?"

"Hop on my back," said the eagle.
"I'll fly you wide and far.
And then you'll see, eventually,
where in the world we are."

Upward and upward the eagle flew.
Armadillo held on tight.
"With my tail-tip curled I'll explore the world
from morning until night!"

Palo Duro Canyon
Amarillo,
TEXAS

PALO DURO CANYON
Near Amarillo and Canyon, Texas
The Lighthouse: The Best-Known Formation
in Palo Duro Canyon State Park

Dear Brillo,
Except for the canyons like
this one here, this land is
flat, flat, flat! And
an Armadillo near
Amarillo should wear
a scarf and hat!
Love,
Sasparillo

POST CARD

BRILLO ARMADILLO
PHILADELPHIA ZOO
CHILDREN'S ZOO
3400 W. GIRARD AVE.
PHILADELPHIA, PA
19104

Armadillo looked down below and asked,
"Where in the world *are* we?"
"We're over a prairie, and in the distance,
that's Amarillo you see.

"We've flown over the prairie.
We've flown over a town.
Amarillo means yellow, my dear little fellow,
and the prairie's all yellow and brown!"

"I see Amarillo," said Armadillo.
"Could we see all Texas, though?
And if we fly *higher* up into the sky,
could we see New Mexico?

"Or if we fly *higher* up into the sky,
could we see the entire earth?"
"Well, certainly, surely, if you hold on securely,
we'll try!" cried the eagle with mirth.

"*Amarillo*'s a *city?*" asked Armadillo.
To this the eagle replied,
"Yes, Amarillo's a city in *Texas*,
the *state* where we reside.

"And Texas is in the *United States*,
our *country* wide and dear,
on the *North American continent*,
which is on the *earth*, a sphere.

"This sphere is called a *planet*,
of nine we are just one,
and as we converse, in the *universe*,
these planets turn round the sun."

Armadillo held tightly to Eagle's neck,
afraid of a long, long fall.
From over his shoulder, with the air getting colder,
this is what he saw.

They flew so high up into the sky
that Texas they saw below—
the part they call the Panhandle—
and the state of New Mexico.

"With my tail-tip curled I'll explore the world!"
Armadillo said to his friend.
Through the clouds they twirled, in the wind
they whirled, and up they were hurled again!

And when they looked up they could see into space.
They'd flown up into thin air.
"It's hard to breathe here! I'd like to leave here!
Eagle, homeward let's repair!"

"We're very high now," said Eagle,
"on the edge of air and space.
The atmosphere's ending, we should be descending,
but what a remarkable place!

"There must be a way to fly higher up,
bringing some air aboard.
Perhaps we should travel to Cape Canaveral,"
Eagle said as she soared.

As they spoke of Cape Canaveral—
the rocket-launching place—
a shuttle took off with a roar of fire
and headed out toward space.

Eagle had a brilliant thought
and whistled a happy tune.
"Let's hitch a trip on this rocket ship
and fly up to the moon!"

With a burst of speed the eagle flew
in the path of the rocket ship.
It took her and Armadillo aboard
and continued on its trip.

The higher they flew, the farther they saw—
Louisiana and Arkansas!
And there were some other countries below—
they could see Cuba and Mexico!

The spaceship then zoomed so high up
that Armadillo could not tell
where a country began or ended,
or where its borders fell.

The earth was now so far away—
so very, very far.
"I'm wondering," said Armadillo,
"where in the world we are."

"We're *out* of this world," said the eagle
to the armadillo, her friend.
"Ten miles from earth starts the universe
right at the atmosphere's end."

From space the earth was a big round ball,
with swirling clouds of white
against a deep-blue background,
like the blue-black sky at night.

Planets shone around them,
reflecting starlike light.
In that silent room floating in the dark,
they traveled through the night.

the earth rose on the horizon.
They sat and gazed at their far-off home—
watched earth-set and earth-risin'.

Armadillo said, "I'm homesick.
Hey, Eagle, let's go back.
Let's go back down to our yellow town,
away from this blue and black."

The rocket began a downward arc,
then flew over land and sea.
The adventurous pair flew through the air
to their home by the yellow prairie.

He'd wondered where in the world he was,
and now Armadillo knew.
He said, "I know where, in the scheme of things,
I am, Eagle, thanks to you!

"I now live near Amarillo,
a city that's rather small,
which is in the state of Texas,
one of fifty states in all,

"in the United States of America,
the country of my birth,
on the North American continent,
in the world, on planet earth.

"In all, there are nine planets,
and earth is only one,
and as we converse, in the universe,
eight planets besides this one
warmly, hotly, coldly, coolly
revolve around the sun."

Think and Respond

1. Why does Armadillo go on his journey? What does he learn?

2. How would the story be different if the author, Lynne Cherry, had not used rhyming words?

3. How do the postcard illustrations add to the story?

4. On the last page of the story, Armadillo tells exactly where he is in the **universe**. Where are you? Give your location exactly, beginning with your school.

5. Give an example of a reading strategy you used as you read this selection. How was it helpful?

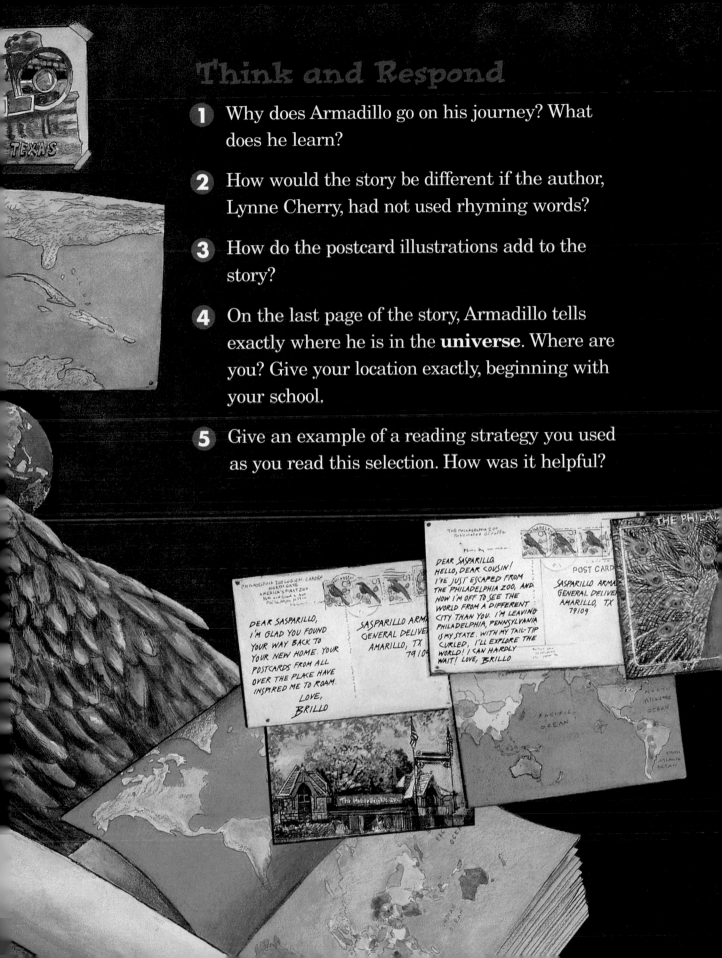

PHILADELPHIA ZOO LOGICAL GARDEN
NORTH GATE
AMERICA'S FIRST ZOO
Now and Giant's Ave
Philadelphia PA 19104

DEAR SASPARILLO,
I'M GLAD YOU FOUND
YOUR WAY BACK TO
YOUR NEW HOME. YOUR
POSTCARDS FROM ALL
OVER THE PLACE HAVE
INSPIRED ME TO ROAM.
LOVE,
BRILLO

SASPARILLO ARMA
GENERAL DELIVE
AMARILLO, TX
79 10

THE PHILADELPHIA ZOO
Reticulated Giraffe

DEAR SASPARILLO
HELLO, DEAR COUSIN!
I'VE JUST ESCAPED FROM
THE PHILADELPHIA ZOO, AND
NOW I'M OFF TO SEE THE
WORLD FROM A DIFFERENT
CITY THAN YOU. I'M LEAVING
PHILADELPHIA, PENNSYLVANIA
IS MY STATE. WITH MY TAIL-TIP
CURLED, I'LL EXPLORE THE
WORLD! I CAN HARDLY
WAIT! LOVE, BRILLO

POST CARD

SASPARILLO ARMA
GENERAL DELIVE
AMARILLO, TX
79109

THE PHILAD

The Philadelphia Zoo

Meet the Author
and Illustrator
Lynne Cherry

Lynne Cherry enjoys watching animals and nature. Her art shows the beauty she sees in life. By traveling and learning about other places, authors can get new ideas. Here is a passport with more information about Lynne Cherry.

PASSPORT
Lynne Cherry

Number: J00932A09 Armadillo

Name: Lynne Cherry

Address: Washington, D.C., and Maryland

Country of birth: United States of America

Place of birth: Philadelphia, PA, U.S.A.

Date of birth: January 5, 1952

Profession: Author and illustrator of children's picture books

Visit *The Learning Site!*
www.harcourtschool.com

Mapping the World

by Barbara Taylor

You have probably seen many flat maps of the world, with the Earth's land and sea stretched out on one page or sheet. But because the Earth is round, the only really accurate map of the world is a globe—a round model of the Earth.

Globes show us the true size and shape of our land and sea. They are also tilted at a slight angle because the Earth leans slightly to one side. But globes are hard to carry around. They cannot be folded up and put in a pocket like a flat map, so we use flat maps more often.

Old Maps

Hundreds of years ago most people believed that the Earth was flat, like a giant tabletop. They thought they would fall off the edge if they sailed far enough out to sea. This map was drawn about 500 years ago.

Although it is not accurate, it is easy to recognize the shapes of the different land areas. Can you recognize parts of Europe and Africa?

Try This!

Have you ever had to wrap up a round birthday present? Try covering a ball with a single sheet of paper and not leaving any gaps. You can see how hard it is to make a flat map of the Earth.

Think and Respond

When is a flat map better than a globe?

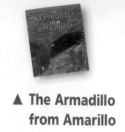
Making Connections

Compare Texts

1. How might Armadillo feel differently about earth after his journey? Tell why.

2. Give examples of fantasy and fact from "The Armadillo from Amarillo."

3. In what ways are "The Armadillo from Amarillo" and "Mapping the World" alike and unlike?

4. Think of another fantasy story you have read. Does that story also give information, as "The Armadillo from Amarillo" does? Explain.

5. Which topic would you rather research to learn more about—your city, your state, your country, your continent, or the universe? Explain the reasons for your choice.

Write a Poem

Writing CONNECTION

"The Armadillo from Amarillo" is written in rhyme. Think about a subject you would like to write a rhyming poem about, such as a favorite place or animal. Write to express your thoughts and feelings in rhyme and rhythmic language.

Jot down rhyming words for your poem in a graphic organizer like this one.

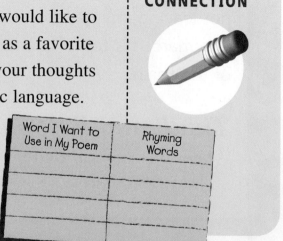

Word I Want to Use in My Poem	Rhyming Words

Create a Diagram or Model

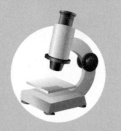

In "The Armadillo from Amarillo," Armadillo learns that earth is one of nine planets that revolve around the sun. Find out the names of all nine planets, their order from nearest to farthest away from the sun, and their order from smallest to largest. Show the information by drawing a diagram or constructing a model. Include a brief written explanation of your diagram or model.

Design Postcards

Armadillo sends many postcards to his cousin Brillo. Design at least one postcard that someone who lived long ago in your community might have sent to a friend. On one side, draw a picture that shows something about your area at a time in the past. You might use your social studies text or sources such as old photographs and newspapers. On the other side of the card, write a brief description of the picture and the time period it shows.

Cause and Effect

Focus Skill

You know that a **cause** is the reason something happens. An **effect** is the result of an action or event.

Sometimes a cause has more than one effect.

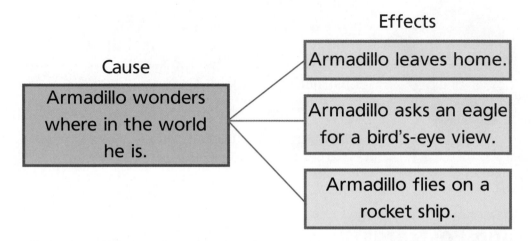

Effects

Cause

| Armadillo wonders where in the world he is. |

Armadillo leaves home.

Armadillo asks an eagle for a bird's-eye view.

Armadillo flies on a rocket ship.

Sometimes there is more than one cause for an effect.

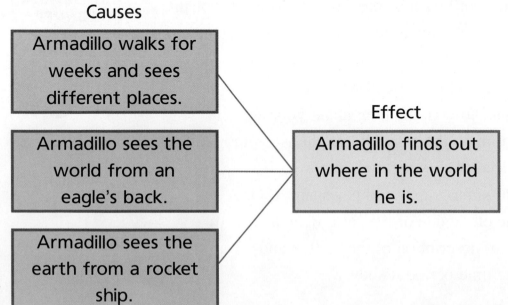

Causes

Armadillo walks for weeks and sees different places.

Armadillo sees the world from an eagle's back.

Armadillo sees the earth from a rocket ship.

Effect

Armadillo finds out where in the world he is.

Visit *The Learning Site!*
www.harcourtschool.com

See *Skills* and *Activities*

Test Prep
Cause and Effect

> One day a traveling lizard came upon a rabbit who looked very sad. The rabbit told the lizard, "Usually the crops in the farmer's fields grow well. The soil is rich, and there has always been enough sunshine and enough rain. But now there has been no rain for many weeks. Soon the crops will turn brown and dry up."
>
> Just then, the lizard felt a drop hit her head. It began to rain. The lizard got wet, but she was glad that the crops would be saved.

1. **The story states three reasons that—**

   A the lizard is traveling

   B the rabbit looks sad

   C the crops usually grow well

   D the lizard got wet

   Tip
   Look back at the story to see how many reasons it gives for each of the choices.

2. **What does the rabbit say the effect will be since there has been no rain for many weeks?**

   F It will begin to rain. The crops will be saved.

   G The crops will get enough sun. They will grow well.

   H The soil will be rich. There will be plenty to eat.

   J The crops will turn brown. The crops will dry up.

   Tip
   Be sure that both of the effects in the answer you choose are caused by not having rain.

Vocabulary Power

solar wind

particles

force

fluorescent

nucleus

loops

What are comets? Where do they come from? These questions were like riddles to people long ago. Here are some other science questions and riddles you can try to answer.

QUESTION: Can a **solar wind** blow your umbrella inside out?

ANSWER: No. The solar wind is magnetic material that flows from the sun. It is a stream of tiny **particles**, or bits too small to see or feel. The **force**, or energy, of the solar wind doesn't reach the ground on Earth. However, it is a very strong wind, causing comets' tails to move and change shape.

400

QUESTION: How is a TV screen like a firefly?

ANSWER: Both are **fluorescent**, or bright and glowing. TV screens are coated with a special material that glows. Fireflies glow because of something natural that takes place in their bodies.

QUESTION: How is the head of a comet like the center of a raindrop?

ANSWER: Both can be called a **nucleus**. The head of a comet is the nucleus that is pulled in a huge oval as it **loops** around the sun. When water gathers around a particle to form a raindrop, the particle is also called a nucleus.

Vocabulary–Writing CONNECTION

At school crossings, traffic signs are often painted **fluorescent** yellow. Write a paragraph telling what you think of this, and where else fluorescent paint could be useful.

Genre

Expository
Nonfiction

**Expository nonfiction
explains information
and ideas.**

In this selection, look for

- **illustrations with
captions and labels.**

- **sections divided by
headings.**

VISITORS FROM SPACE

by Jeanne Bendick

illustrated by David Schleinkofer

Look! A Comet

This is what a big, bright comet looks like in the sky. (top right)

Long ago, people thought a comet was a warning that something terrible was going to happen on Earth. It might be an earthquake, a flood, or maybe a war. Why else would a flaming ball suddenly appear in the sky?

Today we know much more about comets. A comet is not a warning of bad things to come. And we know that comets do not appear suddenly. We just don't notice them until they are near the Sun.

Where Do Comets Come From?

Astronomers are scientists who study the planets and stars. They think that comets are made of bits of rock, dust, ice, and gas that were left over when the *Solar System* formed about $4\frac{1}{2}$ billion years ago. The Solar System is the Sun and its family of planets and moons.

Scientists think that far out in space, out past the farthest planet from our Sun, there is a huge cloud of comets wrapped around our Solar System. There may be billions of comets there, moving around like a giant swarm of bees.

The Oort cloud may be like a giant shell around the Solar System. It was named after a Dutch astronomer, Jan H. Oort.

The Sun's gravity pulls the planets inward. At the same time, the planets' own energy of motion is trying to fling them off into space. These two forces balance exactly.

A Comet Starts Its Travels

Once in a while, some faraway star gives a sudden push or pull that can yank a comet out of the comet cloud. The comet may shoot off into space. Or it may start moving through the Solar System, toward the Sun.

Everything in the Solar System is connected to the Sun by a **force** you cannot see. This force is called *gravity*.

The Sun's gravity pulls on the planets and their moons. It pulls on the flying rocks in the Solar System called the *asteroids*. It pulls on comets. It pulls them all toward the star that is the center of our Solar System. That star is our Sun.

Comets Change

Some comets look like fuzzy balls.
Some comets look like long-haired stars.
A comet starts out as a ball of frozen gases.
One astronomer calls comets "dirty snowballs."

That dirty snowball is the *nucleus* of the comet. It is the seed around which the rest of the comet grows. It may be a big seed—a mile or even a few miles wide.

As the comet comes closer to the hot Sun, the ice begins to melt. The frozen gases spread into a misty cloud around the nucleus. That cloud is called the *coma*. The coma may be half a million miles across.

Part of the coma is pushed behind the comet. A force from the Sun called the *solar wind* blows this *tail* out behind the comet.

Most comets grow two tails or more. One tail is gas. It is straight and long—maybe 10 million miles long.

The other tails are shorter and curved. They are made of dust.

The tails of a comet always point away from the Sun. After the comet *loops* around the Sun, the solar wind blows the tail out in front of the comet.

The coma is blown away from the Sun, forming gas tails and dust tails.

dust tail

gas tail

Mercury

Venus

Earth

Mars

What Makes a Comet Glow?

Out in space, comets are dark. They have no light of their own.

As they approach the Sun they begin to glow. The icy particles reflect the sunlight.

Comets reflect sunlight even at night. Reflected sunlight also makes our Moon and the planets shine. Only stars have their own light.

Something else makes comets glow. The gas in the coma soaks up some of the sunlight. It becomes like the gas in a fluorescent light bulb. It glows.

About Orbits

The planets move around the Sun in regular paths, called *orbits*. The orbit of a planet is almost round. When a planet orbits the Sun once, it is a *year* on that planet.

Comets also move in orbits around the Sun. Their orbits are shaped more like eggs. These orbits are called *ellipses* [i•lip´sēz]. Comet orbits may be really long, if the comet starts far out in space.

Some comets take thousands or even millions of years to complete their orbits. Other comets take only a few years. Their orbits might crisscross the orbits of the planets. The time it takes a comet to complete its orbit is called the comet's *period*.

Comets move fast. But they seem to almost stand still in the sky for many nights in a row. They do not seem to move because they are so far away. Doesn't the Moon seem to stand still, too? You have to watch it for a long time to see that it is moving.

A comet's orbit is usually an ellipse.

The Most Famous Comet

Certain comets appear in the sky again and again. We can predict when they will come. These comets are usually given names. Comets are usually named for the people who saw them first.

The most famous comet is called Halley's Comet. We see it about every 76 years, when it comes closest to the Sun. Its period is 76 years.

Halley's Comet passed us in 1985–86. It will come again in 2060. How old will you be then?

This scientist uses a huge dirty snowball to teach students about comets.

What Happens to Comets?

When comets come close to the Sun, the Sun boils away some of the gas in the coma and tail. Bits of dust and rock are blown away from the nucleus. This leaves a trail of comet matter along the comet's orbit. Those pieces, called *meteoroids*, keep on orbiting.

When the Earth passes through their orbit, the meteoroids glow. That's because the Earth is wrapped in a blanket of air called the *atmosphere*. When the meteoroids enter the atmosphere, air particles rub against them. The meteoroids get hotter and hotter until they start to burn. Then they are called *meteors*.

Some people call meteors "shooting stars" or "falling stars." They are not shooting or falling stars. Stars don't fall. You are seeing meteors.

Think and Respond

1 How are comets different from planets?

2 What is the purpose of the words in red letters at the tops of some pages?

3 What effect does the solar wind have on comets?

4 If you could talk with the author, what question would you ask her? Why would you ask this question?

5 What reading strategies did you use to help you understand information in "Visitors from Space"?

Meet the Author

Jeanne Bendick

I have written many, many books. A list of my book titles would stretch on for two or three pages. Most of them are beginning books on science for young readers.

I am not a scientist, though. I am a writer who enjoys learning about a difficult science topic. First, I try to explain a new topic in simple words so that I can understand it. Then, I feel I can write about it for young people.

Through my books, I hope readers will see that science is part of everyday life. I also hope my books will make children ask questions and try to find answers. I think questions are more important than answers. Curiosity about our world is wonderful!

Visit *The Learning Site!*
www.harcourtschool.com

Making Connections

Compare Texts

1 Why does the selection "Visitors from Space" belong in a theme about exploring and celebrating our world?

2 Why are the illustrations for this nonfiction selection mostly diagrams and drawings instead of photographs?

3 Why does the author compare the glow of a coma to a fluorescent light bulb? Why does she compare a comet's movement with the moon's?

4 Compare and contrast "Visitors from Space" with "Rocking and Rolling."

5 After reading "Visitors from Space," what other questions do you have about our solar system?

Write a Song

"**V**isitors from Space" tells how a comet forms and begins its journey around the sun. Think about what you would like to say in the form of a song about a comet. Write to express your thoughts, and set them to music.

Plan your song in a web like this one. You may write a poem and make up your own tune, or write new words for a song you know, such as "Twinkle, Twinkle, Little Star."

Writing CONNECTION

COMET

Give a Demonstration

"Visitors from Space" describes how comets and the moon seem to stand still in the sky, even though they are moving. When we observe the sun over the period of a day, it appears to move across the sky, rising in the east and setting in the west. Do research to find out if the sun is actually moving. Give a demonstration with models of the sun and Earth to show your research.

Science CONNECTION

Make an Internet Guide

In "Visitors from Space," you learned that Halley's Comet last passed Earth in 1985–1986. Photographs of the comet were taken from the spacecraft *Giotto* and from Earth. Do an Internet search to find photographs of Halley's Comet. Take notes on the photographs you find, and record the addresses of the websites. Then write an Internet guide that lists the addresses and describes each site.

Social Studies/Science CONNECTION

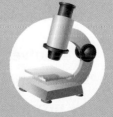

Locate Information

How does ice cause a comet to glow? You can find the answer in "Visitors from Space." Follow these steps to practice **locating information** in textbooks and other nonfiction books.

Look at the table of contents. Locate the number of the page that "Visitors from Space" begins on. Turn to that page.

The selection is divided into sections that are short chapters. Read all of the headings. In which section might you find the answer?

Under the heading "What Makes a Comet Glow?" look for information about ice.

You've found this sentence: "The icy particles reflect the sunlight." Use the glossary to check the pronunciation and meaning of *particles*.

Visit *The Learning Site!*
www.harcourtschool.com

See *Skills* and *Activities*

Test Prep
Locate Information

▶ **This is an index from a book about comets. Use this to answer Numbers 1 and 2.**

Index
Astronomers..3,7,14,27
Coma...............10,11,29
Gravity................5,8,25
Nucleus...............11,12
Period.......................19
Solar wind...........14,17

1. **You can find information about solar wind on pages—**

   A 26 and 30

   B 11 and 12

   C 1, 4, 9, 24, and 28

   D 14 and 17

Tip

Look up *solar wind* in the index to locate the correct page numbers.

2. **Where should a listing be added for orbit?**

   F before astronomers

   G between gravity and nucleus

   H between nucleus and period

   J after solar wind

Tip

Remember that an index is arranged alphabetically.

Writer's Handbook

Contents

Planning your Writing

Purposes for Writing

There are many different purposes for writing. You might be asked to write **to inform, to respond to something you read, to entertain or express feelings,** or **to persuade.** Sometimes you may write for more than one purpose. For example, when writing a friendly letter, you may write to inform the reader about an event and to express your feelings about the event. Before you write, it is important that you think about the task, the audience, and the purpose for writing. Ask yourself these questions:

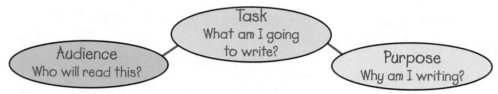

Remember as you are writing to be creative and have fun with your topic. Place yourself in the place of your audience and ask yourself, "What can I write about this topic that will excite my audience?"

Expository Writing

The purpose for expository writing is to inform. This kind of writing explains something. Examples of expository writing are how-to essays, descriptive paragraphs, and research reports.

Sample prompt: *Explain how to get to your house from your school.*

Tips for Expository Writing

- Write a topic sentence that tells the main idea or what you are explaining.
- Organize the information into paragraphs that tell about one idea.
- Use vivid, descriptive language and specific details to convey your interest in the topic to your readers.

Literary Response

When you write to respond to something you have read, your purpose is to show that you understand the passage or selection.

Tips for Literary Response

- Write a topic sentence that answers the question.
- Use your own experience and details from the selection to support your topic sentence.
- Restate your main idea in the conclusion.

Expressive Writing

The purpose for expressive writing is to share your feelings or to entertain. Sometimes expressive writing describes something. Examples of expressive writing are personal narratives, stories, and poems.

Sample prompt: *There are many things to do on a rainy day. Think about what you would do on a rainy day. Now write a story about what you did on a rainy day.*

Tips for Expressive Writing

- Introduce yourself or your characters.
- Use your personal voice to describe what you are writing about.
- Include as many details about what you or your characters see, hear, touch, taste, and smell to draw your reader into the story.
- Have an ending that makes sense.

Persuasive Writing

The purpose of persuasive writing is to persuade readers to agree with your opinions or to take action.

Sample prompt: *Imagine that you want to convince your parents to let you have a sleep over. Write a persuasive paragraph that gives reasons why having a sleep over is a good idea.*

Tips for Persuasive Writing

- Have an interesting beginning that explains your opinion.
- Give at least three reasons why you feel the way you do.
- In your conclusion, restate your opinion or ask your reader to take action.

Try This

What would be the purpose for each of these kinds of writing: a telephone message, a joke, a recipe, and an advertisement?

The Writing Process

The writing process has five steps. You will go back and forth through these steps as you write.

Prewriting: In this step, you plan what you will write. Identify your purpose and who your audience is. Then choose a topic and organize your information.

Drafting: Write out your ideas in sentences and paragraphs. Follow your prewriting plan.

Revising: Make changes to make your writing easier to understand or more interesting to read.

Proofreading: In this step, check for errors in grammar, spelling, capitalization, and punctuation. Then make a final copy of your work.

Publishing: Choose a way to share your work. You may add pictures or read your writing aloud.

Here is an example, showing how Keesha used the writing process to write a personal narrative.

Prewriting

Keesha was asked to write a personal narrative. Her audience would be her classmates. She remembered the time she broke her leg. Her next step was to write down everything she could remember.

Fell off bicycle.
Broke leg.
Got crutches.
Couldn't get out of a chair.
Couldn't go up and down stairs.
Then learned how to go really
 fast on them.

Drafting

Keesha wrote about the events in the order that they took place. She also thought about details that would describe what happened.

Revising

Keesha made changes to improve her writing. She checked to see whether her ideas were in the right order. She added details and took out unnecessary information. She made a run-on sentence into two separate sentences. Here is her first draft with some changes she made in **blue.**

Proofreading

Keesha looked for mistakes in grammar, spelling, punctuation, and capitalization. The corrections in **red** show the changes she made while proofreading.

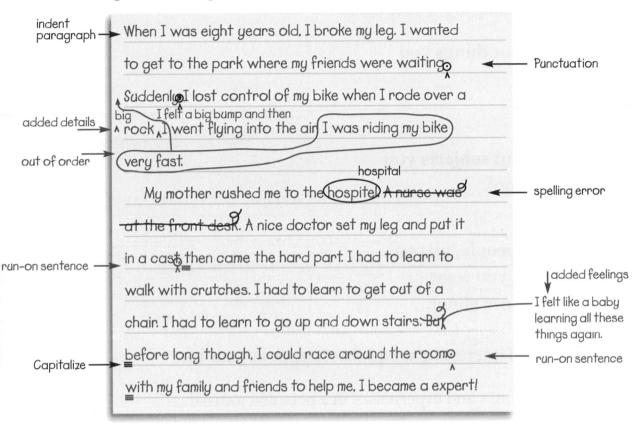

indent paragraph →

Punctuation

added details →

out of order →

spelling error

run-on sentence →

added feelings

run-on sentence

Capitalize →

When I was eight years old, I broke my leg. I wanted to get to the park where my friends were waiting.

Suddenly I lost control of my bike when I rode over a big rock. I felt a big bump and then I went flying into the air. I was riding my bike very fast.

My mother rushed me to the hospital. A nurse was at the front desk. A nice doctor set my leg and put it in a cast then came the hard part. I had to learn to walk with crutches. I had to learn to get out of a chair. I had to learn to go up and down stairs. But before long though, I could race around the room. I felt like a baby learning all these things again. With my family and friends to help me, I became a expert!

Publishing

Keesha decided to read her story aloud to the class. She brought her crutches to school. She showed how hard it was to get out of a chair. Then she answered questions.

Try This

Imagine you are writing a story about a time you tried something new. Decide what your purpose and audience will be. Then think of interesting ways to publish your story.

How to Get Ideas

Once you know your purpose and audience, here are ways to get ideas:

Keep **lists** in a Reading log or idea bank.

- **Think about things you like to do.**

- **Think about subjects you like in school.**

- **Research people, places, and things you want to know more about.**

> ### Things I Like
> arts and crafts
> sports
> board games
> reading

> ### Interesting Lessons in School
> air pressure experiment
> estimation games
> mock trial in social studies

> ### Things I want to learn more about
> weather forecasting
> Paris, France
> Video games
> art programs on the computer

Keep a **timeline** of interesting things that happen in your life.

- Record feelings and experiences in a personal journal.

- Draw pictures to remind you of memorable events.

- Describe yourself at different times in your life.

Use **freewriting** when you get stuck.

- Start with a topic word or a feeling word.

- Write freely for several minutes. Do not pick your pencil up off the paper.

- Write every thought that comes to your mind. You never know when a good idea will come to you.

When you find an idea you want to write about, you can explore it some more, using an idea web. Janna made a web like this one to describe an elephant that she saw at the zoo.

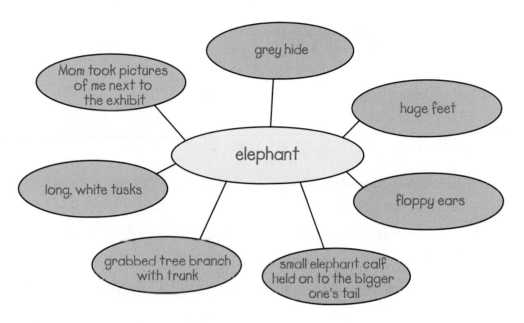

Guidelines for Making an Idea Web:

- Write a word as your starting point. Circle it.

- Around it, write ideas that pop into your head.

- Circle each idea.

Try This

Select an object that is important to you. Imagine that you will write a paragraph about it. Make a web like the web Janna made, but write your object in the center circle. In the outside circles, write all your ideas about the object.

Library Resources

You can find books, magazines, videos, audiocassettes, and even games in a library. The library lends all of these items free to the people who live in the area. All you need to do is ask for a library card.

The books in a library are arranged so that you can find what you need easily. **Fiction books** are arranged in alphabetical order by the last names of the authors. **Nonfiction books** are grouped according to subject. **Reference books** such as dictionaries, atlases, almanacs, and encyclopedias, can be found in a special section of the library.

Libraries have card catalogs to help you find books. A card catalog has a card for every book in the library. These cards are put in alphabetical order in drawers. An **electronic card catalog** has the same information, but it is on a computer.

At the computer, you can type **keywords,** such as the name of an author, the title of a book, or the subject of a book. Then the computer will provide a list of titles. Each **entry,** or listing, includes a short summary of the book.

J974.45.C
Chandler, Timothy.
<u>Pioneer Life in America.</u>
Nonfic.
Children's Room
©1990

A close look at the everyday life of pioneers in this country

J971.04F
Fellers, Frances.
<u>Life in the West.</u> Nonfic.
Children's Room
©1994

Struggles of the early settlers in America's Western states

Using a Dictionary

A **dictionary** is a book that gives the meanings of words. It also shows how to say them.

Words in a dictionary are listed in alphabetical order. At the top of each dictionary page are **guide words.** The first guide word is the first word on the page. The next guide word is the last word on the page. Use the guide words to help you find the page that lists the word you need.

A **pronunciation key** can be found on every other page. The key shows the letters and symbols used in the pronunciation of each entry. Then it gives sample words to show how to pronounce each sound.

The words in dark type on each dictionary page are called **entry words.**

The special spelling shows how to say the word aloud. The way a word sounds when it is said aloud is called its **pronunciation.**

The letter or letters after the pronunciation tell the **part of speech.** Most dictionaries use abbreviations for this.

The meaning of a word is called the **definition.** When a word has more than one definition, the definitions are numbered. The most common definition comes first.

gav • el [gav' əl] *n.* A small wooden mallet used by a person in charge of a meeting to call for attention or order.

ga • votte [gə vot'] *n.* A 17th-century French dance, like the minuet but somewhat quicker.

Ga • wain [gä' win] *n.* One of the knights of the Round Table, nephew of King Arthur.

gawk [gôk] *informal* **1** *v.* To stare stupidly; gape. **2** *n.* An awkward, clumsy person.

gawk • y [gô 'kē] *adj.* **gawk • i • er, gawk • i • est** Awkward or clumsy. —**gawk' i • ly** *adv.* —**gawk' i • ness** *n.*

gaze [gāz] *v.* **gazed, gaz • ing,** *n.* **1** *v.* To look steadily; stare. **2** *n.* A steady or fixed look. —**gaz' er** *n.*

a	at	i	it	o͝o	book	oi	oil
ā	ape	ī	ice	o͞o	cool	ou	out
â	care	o	odd	u	up	ng	long
ä	father	ō	old	û	burn	th	thin
e	end	ô	order	yo͞o	use	th	this
ē	equal					zh	vision
ə = a in *above*		e in *taken*		i in *pencil*		o in *lemon*	u in *circus*

Pronunciation Key

Try This

Play a game with a friend where you each race to look up the same word in a dictionary. The person who writes the word, the page number, and the guide words first wins.

Using a Thesaurus

A **thesaurus** is a book that lists words and their synonyms and antonyms.

Synonyms are words that have almost the same meanings. **Antonyms** are words with opposite meanings. **Entry words** are listed in alphabetical order. **Guide words** at the top of each page show the first and last words on that page.

A thesaurus is an important tool because it can help you choose the right word to use.

The word **broken** is an **entry word.** Entry words are in dark type. They are listed in alphabetical order in the thesaurus.

The abbreviation *adj.* tells the part of speech.
Abbreviations
n.	noun	*v.*	verb
adj.	adjective	*adv.*	adverb
prep.	preposition		

broken *adj.* Not in good condition; not working; damaged: The *broken* cup lay in many pieces.

cracked Broken but not completely falling apart: The *cracked* mirror still hung on the wall.

crushed Broken completely by being pressed between two things: A *crushed* tomato was at the bottom of the grocery bag.

ANTONYMS: fixed, mended, repaired

These are **synonyms** for the word *broken*. Read each definition to find the word that has the best meaning for you.

Using an Atlas

An **atlas** is a book of maps. A world atlas has maps of every country in the world. Some atlases have maps of only one country. Different kinds of maps show different facts about places.

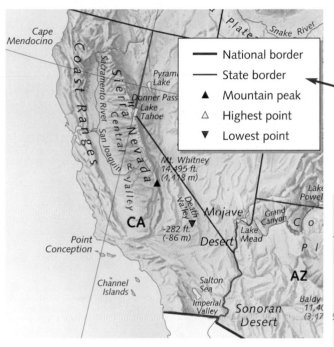

This is a *relief* map. It shows where in California there are mountains, valleys, and bodies of water. Colors are used to show how high the land is. The **legend** tells you what the symbols mean.

———	National border
———	State border
▲	Mountain peak
△	Highest point
▼	Lowest point

★	State capital
■	Metropolitan area

This map shows the names of some cities in California. The legend, or **map key,** tells you that the city with a star next to its name is the state capital. On the map, the star is next to Sacramento, the capital of California.

Try This

Look in an atlas for other maps of California with different information than the maps shown here. What types of information do they present? What might the information on those maps be useful for? Make a list of the different types of maps you find and what they might be useful for.

Book Parts

Books are organized to help you find information.

Front of the Book

- The **title page** shows the name of the book, the author, and the name of the company that made, or published, the book. It also says where the book was published.

- The **copyright page** tells you in what year the book was made.

- The **table of contents** lists the names of the chapters or units. It tells on which page each chapter or unit begins.

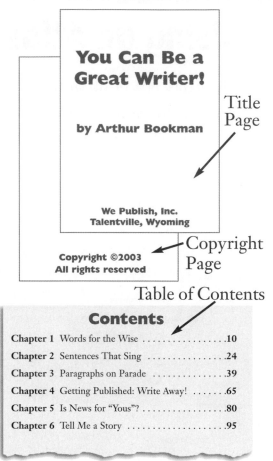

Title Page

Copyright Page

Table of Contents

Contents

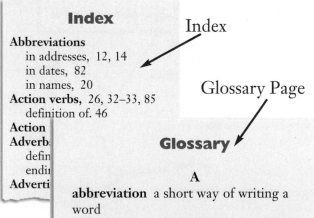

Index

Glossary Page

Back of the Book

- The **glossary** gives the meanings of important words in the book. The glossary is arranged in alphabetical order.

- The **index** is a list of topics in the book. Page numbers next to each word tell where in the book you can find that information.

Using an Encyclopedia

An **encyclopedia** is a book or a set of books that gives information about many different subjects. In a printed set of encyclopedias, each **volume,** or book, has one or more letters on its spine (or side). The letters go from A to Z. Sometimes each book has a number as well. A CD-ROM version of a printed encyclopedia will sometimes have all the information from all the volumes on one disc!

All the subjects in any kind of encyclopedia are arranged in alphabetical order. If you wanted to look up ponds in a printed encyclopedia, you would look in volume 8, *P.*

Articles give facts about the topics in an encyclopedia.

This **guide word** tells you the last topic on this page.

Pony

Pond is a small, quiet body of water that is shallow enough for sunlight to reach the bottom. The sunlight allows plants to grow across the bottom of the pond, from shore to shore. In most cases, ponds are the home for many kinds of animals and plants. The wind and streams carry in eggs and seeds that grow into different forms of life. Pond animals include birds, fish, frogs, insects and turtles. Many ponds have plants that grow under the water and leafy plants that float on top of it.

See also **Marsh; Swamp**

Cross-references tell you where to find articles on a similar topic.

Try This

Look up a keyword in a CD-ROM encyclopedia and in a print encyclopedia. Which do you think gives more information? Which do you prefer to use? Why?

Note Taking

A good way to remember information you read is to **take notes.** You can look at your notes when you write a report or study for a test.

Putting your notes on cards can help you organize ideas and details. Make a separate card for each main idea. Then you will be able to put the cards in order in different ways if you need to. This can be useful if you are writing a report.

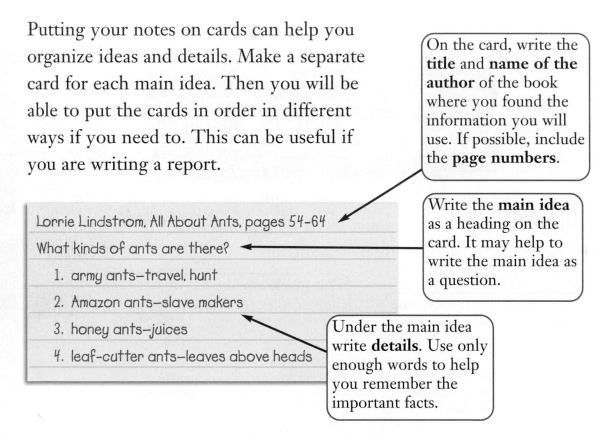

On the card, write the **title** and **name of the author** of the book where you found the information you will use. If possible, include the **page numbers**.

Write the **main idea** as a heading on the card. It may help to write the main idea as a question.

Lorrie Lindstrom, All About Ants, pages 54-64

What kinds of ants are there?

1. army ants—travel, hunt

2. Amazon ants—slave makers

3. honey ants—juices

4. leaf-cutter ants—leaves above heads

Under the main idea write **details**. Use only enough words to help you remember the important facts.

Note Taking with Graphic Organizers

Sometimes it helps to use a graphic organizer when you take notes. A **K-W-L** chart is a good chart for notetaking. The chart has three columns.

- Write what you **know** about the subject in the **K** column. Do this before you read.

- Write questions about what you **want** to find out in the **W** column.

- Write what you **learn** in the **L** column. Do this as you are reading.

Ants		
K	W	L
small black or red insects	What kinds of ants are there?	army ants: travel most of the time
live in large groups	What is special about each kind?	Amazon ants: kidnap other ants
very strong		honey ants: collect juice

A **web** is another helpful graphic organizer to use when you are taking notes. A web shows how facts or ideas are connected.

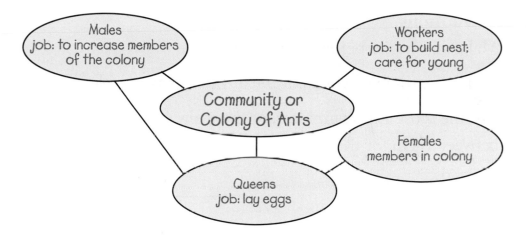

A **Venn diagram** helps you compare two things. This Venn diagram shows how ants and termites are alike and how they are different.

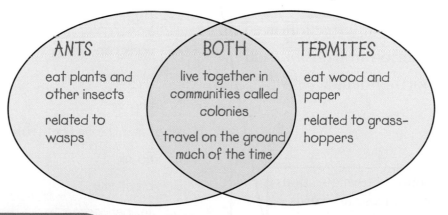

Try This

Think about two of your favorite things to do during your free time. On a sheet of paper, make a Venn diagram and use it to compare and contrast these two activities.

Outlining

Outlining is a good way to organize information. When you read, an outline can help you keep track of the main ideas and the details in an article or book. When you write, an outline can help you plan your ideas into paragraphs.

Tips for Outlining

- Make an outline before you write.

- Write the topic of your outline at the top as its title.

- List the most important ideas, or the main ideas. Leave space between them for the details.

- Put a Roman numeral followed by a period in front of each main idea.

- List supporting details below each main idea.

- Put a capital letter followed by a period in front of each supporting detail.

This outline uses questions for main ideas and words and phrases for supporting details. You can also create a **sentence outline** in which all the items are complete sentences.

The Moon

I.   What is a moon?
   A.   a satellite that orbits a planet
   B.   Earth's one satellite

II.   What does a moon look like?
   A.   rocky and gray
   B.   high mountains
   C.   craters

III.   What is it like on Earth's moon?
   A.   no air
   B.   black sky
   C.   temperature
      1. very hot
      2. very cold
   D.   little gravity

Here is a report about the moon that was written using the outline. Compare the outline and the report.

The Moon

Since ancient times, people have told stories and sung songs about the moon. In fact, a moon is something in space that circles around, or orbits, a planet. Some planets have twenty moons or more. Earth has just one.

The surface of the moon is rocky and gray. It is covered with a layer of fine dust. On the moon, you can see high mountains. Many of these were volcanoes at one time. There are also craters, or holes, on the moon. Some craters are less than one foot across. Other craters are as much as seven hundred miles across. Flying masses of space matter, called meteorites, probably crashed into the moon and made these craters.

A visit to the moon would be a strange experience! There is no air, or atmosphere, on the moon. That means sound cannot travel. On the moon, the sky is always black. Even during the day you can see the stars. The temperature on the moon is very hot or very cold. One place has temperatures above the boiling point of water. Another place has temperatures hundreds of degrees below zero. Finally, the pull of gravity is much less on the moon. If you weigh 90 pounds on Earth, you will weigh only 15 pounds on the moon. Just think how high you could jump!

The first paragraph explains **what a moon is.**

The second paragraph explains **how the moon looks.**

The third paragraph explains **what it is like to be on the moon.**

Try This

Make an outline of what you do on a Saturday or Sunday. Divide the outline into three main sections. List at least 2 supporting details under each main idea. Remember to use Roman numerals and letters to separate the different parts of your outline.

Traits of Good Writing

Writing is like any other skill or activity. It takes time, practice, and effort. There are rules you have to learn and **traits,** or features, of good writing that you will learn to recognize. But once you understand those rules and traits, writing can be a lot of fun. Think about another activity you enjoy. When you did it for the first few times, learning the rules was important. Once you knew the rules, though, you could focus on having fun.

Think about drawing, for example. To draw well, an artist needs to be able to imagine what he wants to draw, sketch it out on whatever he's drawing on, and then add details and maybe colors to make the drawing look real. Very few people can do this well from the beginning. Most artists have to train their imaginations to see things in detail, and train their hands to make the marks and shapes that look like what they're imagining. Creating mental images, sketching, and detail drawing are **traits of good drawing.** They are skills that good artists practice and improve in order to draw well.

Good writing takes practice at these skills, too. This web shows the **traits of good writing.**

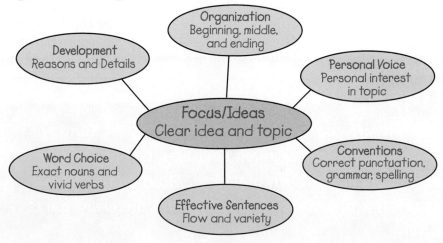

436

Quick Checklist for Good Writers

Good writers practice, practice, practice! As you practice, ask yourself these questions. If you can say "yes" to most of them, you are doing quite well indeed! If you need work in some areas, use the lessons in this handbook. Keep practicing!

✔ **FOCUS/IDEAS** Are my ideas clear? Do I stay on the topic?

✔ **ORGANIZATION** Do I have a clear beginning, middle, and ending? Are similar ideas grouped together in paragraphs?

✔ **DEVELOPMENT** Do I use details and reasons to support my ideas?

✔ **VOICE** Do I seem to care about my topic?

✔ **EFFECTIVE SENTENCES** Do I use a variety of sentence types?

✔ **WORD CHOICE** Do I use exact nouns and vivid verbs?

✔ **CONVENTIONS** Are my spelling, grammar, and punctuation correct?

Try This

Choose a piece of writing from your portfolio. Use the Quick Checklist. What are your strengths? What can you improve? Jot down your ideas in your Writer's Journal.

Using a Rubric

A rubric is a list you can use to check your writing. It spells out the main points of good writing.

Before writing   Use the list to remind you of the traits of good writing.

During writing   Use the list to see how you can improve your drafts.

After writing   Use the list to see if your essay or story has all the points of good writing.

Here is a checklist you can use to self-evaluate your writing.

My Best Score

✓   Do I make the topic and my ideas clear to the reader?

✓   Does my essay move from beginning to the middle to the end smoothly? Is it easy to follow?

✓   Do I support my ideas with specific reasons and details?

✓   Do my words show my interest and knowledge in the topic?

✓   Do I use different kinds of sentences in my essay?

✓   Are my choices of nouns and verbs specific and vivid?

✓   Do I use correct grammar, spelling, and punctuation?

Peer Conferences

You can make your writing better by reading your work to a classmate. **Peer conferences** are a good way to get helpful comments and suggestions.

Here are some questions to ask a friend when you want help with your writing:

1. Is my topic interesting to you? Can you figure out my point of view?

2. Do you understand the order of events? Is there anything I left out?

3. Is this detail important? Should I include it?

4. Can you suggest a better word for_____?

5. Do I have any choppy sentences? Can any sentences be combined?

6. Do I have any run-on sentences?

7. Are there mistakes in spelling, grammar, or punctuation?

Tips for peer conferences:

- Listen carefully to someone else's writing.

- Make suggestions, but don't tell the writer what to do.

- Remember to tell what you like about the writing.

- Be polite and encouraging. Agree or disagree in a pleasant way.

Try This

Write a paragraph about a time you went somewhere new and had a good time. Share your paragraph with a partner, and conduct a peer conference.

Giving an Oral Presentation

One way to share your writing with classmates is to give an oral presentation.

Tips for giving an oral presentation:

1. Write the report on note cards in big print.
2. Practice reading your report aloud in front of a mirror or to a friend.
3. When you speak, look at your audience some of the time. Make motions with your hands, too. This will keep your listeners interested in your presentation.
4. Speak clearly and loudly enough for everyone to hear you. Speak slowly enough for everyone to understand you. Change your tone of voice every now and then to stress important parts of what you read.
5. Make your presentation more interesting by using props. You might use things that describe your topic, such as posters, pictures or charts.
6. When you finish, ask for questions from the audience.

Tips for listeners:

1. Listen politely to the speaker's presentation. Don't talk with your neighbors.
2. Look at the speaker to show your interest.
3. Save your questions for the end. You may also want to add information you have on the topic that might be interesting.

Giving a Multimedia Presentation

You can use different means of communication, such as pictures, videos, music, or drama, when you share a report with your class. This is called a **multimedia presentation.** Here are the steps to follow:

1. Decide which multimedia aids fit your report best. For example, if you are doing a report on state songs, you might bring a CD or cassette tape of music. If you are doing a report on tropical fish, you might bring photos, drawings, videotapes, or maps.

2. Get permission to use equipment that you need, such as a tape recorder or a videotape player. Learn how to operate the equipment ahead of time. If you are presenting your report as a play or skit, ask classmates to assist you by acting out parts.

3. Decide at what time during your presentation you will use the multimedia aids.

4. Organize the spoken part of your presentation. Write notes of what you will say. Practice reading your notes.

5. Invite your classmates to ask questions about your report.

Try This

Imagine that you have been asked to give an oral report about a hobby that you have or a club in which you are involved. Make a list of aids you could use in your presentation.

Using the Glossary

Like a dictionary, this glossary lists words in alphabetical order. To find a word, look it up by its first letter or letters.

To save time, use the **guide words** at the top of each page. These show you the first and last words on the page. Look at the guide words to see if your word falls between them alphabetically.

Here is an example of a glossary entry:

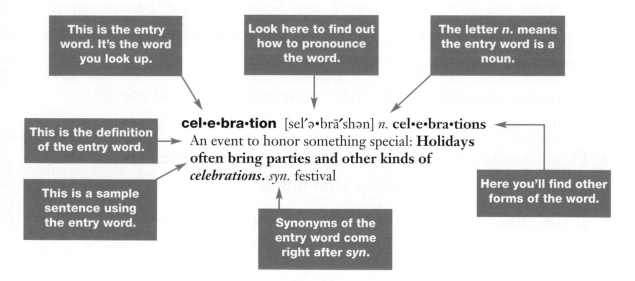

Word Origins

Throughout the glossary, you will find notes about word origins, or how words get started and change. Words often have interesting backgrounds that can help you remember what they mean.

Here is an example of a word origin note:

harvest Until the 1700s, *harvest* named the season we now know as *autumn*. That was the time when many crops were picked.

Pronunciation

The pronunciation in brackets is a respelling that shows how the word is pronounced.

The **pronunciation key** explains what the symbols in a respelling mean. A shortened pronunciation key appears on every other page of the glossary.

PRONUNCIATION KEY*

a	add, map	m	move, seem	u	up, done
ā	ace, rate	n	nice, tin	û(r)	burn, term
â(r)	care, air	ng	ring, song	yo͞o	fuse, few
ä	palm, father	o	odd, hot	v	vain, eve
b	bat, rub	ō	open, so	w	win, away
ch	check, catch	ô	order, jaw	y	yet, yearn
d	dog, rod	oi	oil, boy	z	zest, muse
e	end, pet	ou	pout, now	zh	vision, pleasure
e	equal, tree	o͝o	took, full	ə	the schwa, an
f	fit, half	o͞o	pool, food		unstressed vowel
g	go, log	p	pit, stop		representing the
h	hope, hate	r	run, poor		sound spelled
i	it, give	s	see, pass		*a* in *above*
ī	ice, write	sh	sure, rush		*e* in *sicken*
j	joy, ledge	t	talk, sit		*i* in *possible*
k	cool, take	th	thin, both		*o* in *melon*
l	look, rule	t̶h̶	this, bathe		*u* in *circus*

Other symbols:
- • separates words into syllables
- ′ indicates heavier stress on a syllable
- ′ indicates light stress on a syllable

Abbreviations: *adj.* adjective, *adv.* adverb, *conj.* conjunction, *interj.* interjection, *n.* noun, *prep.* preposition, *pron.* pronoun, *syn.* synonym, *v.* verb

* The Pronunciation Key, adapted entries, and the Short Key that appear on the following pages are reprinted from *HBJ School Dictionary* Copyright © 1990 by Harcourt Brace & Company. Reprinted by permission of Harcourt Brace & Company.

A

ad·mire [ad·mīr′] *v.* **ad·mir·ing** To look upon with pleasure and approval: **Bonnie strolled through the park, *admiring* the rose garden.**

ad·vice [ad·vīs′] *n.* Suggestions or directions on what to do: **Tom asked for *advice* on how to set up his computer.**

a·mount [ə·mount′] *n.* A certain number of: **We saved our money in the bank until we had the *amount* we needed for our trip.** *syn.* quantity

> **Word Origins**
> **amount** *Amount* comes from the Latin *ad montem*, which means "to the mountain," and so "going in an upward direction." As you add up numbers to find the amount, or sum, you are "climbing a mountain" of numbers!

am·ple [am′pəl] *adj.* Enough or more than enough: **We had *ample* food for everyone, so no one went hungry.**

ar·range [ə·rānj′] *v.* **ar·ranged** To place things in a certain order: **Lian *arranged* the books on the shelf from tallest to shortest.** *syn.* organize

auc·tion·eer [ôk′shən·ir′] *n.* A person who sells things at a public sale to people offering the highest prices: **The *auctioneer* spoke very fast as he called out the prices being offered.**

av·er·age [av′rij] *adj.* Usual or ordinary: **Juan is an *average* runner, not unusually fast or slow.**

B

bar·gain [bär′gən] *v.* To work out an agreement about selling or trading something: **Mother had to *bargain* with our neighbor to trade some of our corn for some of his eggs.**

bid [bid] *n.* An offer to pay a certain price for something: **Sally wanted to buy the lamp, so she made a *bid* of five dollars for it.**

boom town [bōom′ toun] *n.* A town that grows quickly and has successful businesses: **This is becoming a *boom town* as more people move in and open new stores.**

bram·ble [bram′bəl] *n.* **bram·bles** A rough and prickly plant, smaller than a tree: **Be careful not to get scratched if you step into the *brambles* growing along the road.**

bramble

brit·tle [brit′əl] *adj.* Easily broken: **This old clay pot is very *brittle*, so handle it carefully.**

can·yon [kan′yən] *n.* A deep valley with high cliffs on both sides: **When you look down into a** *canyon*, **you may see a river running through it.**

canyon

cel·e·bra·tion [sel′ə·brā′shən] *n.* **cel·e·bra·tions** An event to honor something special: **Holidays often bring parties and other kinds of** *celebrations.* *syn.* festival

cher·ish [cher′ish] *v.* **cher·ished** To care about or hold dear: **Helga** *cherished* **the doll her grandmother had given her.**

choice [chois] *n.* **choic·es** What you decide to have or to do: **When you decide what you want to eat and to wear, you are making** *choices.* *syn.* selection

choos·y [choo′zē] *adj.* Very careful about deciding; paying close attention to: **Joan is** *choosy* **about what she wears, so it takes her a long time to dress.** *syn.* fussy

clutch [kluch] *v.* **clutched** To hold onto something tightly: **Larisa** *clutched* **her purse in both hands on the crowded bus.** *syn.* grasp

coast [kōst] *n.* Land that is along the sea: **Cities along the** *coast* **can be reached by ship as well as by train.** *syn.* seashore

Word Origins

coast What does a rib have to do with a coast? In Latin, *costa* means "rib," and people in the past used *coast* to mean "side." People now use *coast* to mean "seashore" or "seaside" because we think of the coast as being the land at the "side" or "edge" of the ocean.

colo·nel [kûr′nəl] *n.* A senior officer in the military: **The** *colonel* **commanded his troops to carry supplies across the river.**

com·bi·na·tion [kom′bə·nā′shən] *n.* **com·bi·na·tions** Something made by putting other things together: **Salads usually are** *combinations* **of different kinds of vegetables or fruits.**

con·grat·u·la·tions [kən·grach′ə·lā′shənz] *n.* Good wishes to someone who has done well: **When our team won the game, the coach gave us his** *congratulations.*

con·ti·nent [kon′tə·nənt] *n.* One of the main areas of land that make up the earth: **The United States is part of the** *continent* **of North America.**

continent

a add	e end	o odd	o͞o pool	oi oil	t̶h̶ this	*a* in *above*
ā ace	ē equal	ō open	u up	ou pout	zh vision	*e* in *sicken*
â care	i it	ô order	û burn	ng ring		ə = *i* in *possible*
ä palm	ī ice	o͝o took	yo͞o fuse	th thin		*o* in *melon*
						u in *circus*

con·verse [kən·vûrs′] *v.* To talk: **If you would like to *converse* with me, call me on the telephone.**

cor·ral [kə·ral′] *n.* A fenced-in space for farm animals: **The cattle were put in a *corral* to keep them from wandering away.** *syn.* pen

coun·cil [koun′səl] *n.* A group of people who meet to talk about something or to make plans: **The *council* met, and its members decided to clean up the park.**

> **Fact File**
> **council** A city *council* is a group of men and women who are chosen by the people of the city. They make laws that help the city run smoothly. The American colonies modeled their first city councils after those in England.

coun·ty [koun′tē] *n.* One of the parts into which a state is divided: **My uncle lives in the same state as I do, but in a different *county*.**

county

cun·ning [kun′ing] *adj.* Crafty or sly: **The *cunning* squirrel took a nut from my plate when I wasn't looking.**

de·light·ed [di·līt′ed] *adj.* Highly pleased: **Maya was *delighted* to get so many wonderful gifts.**

dread·ful [dred′fəl] *adj.* Awful; very bad: **The *dreadful* tornado struck the town with a roar.** *syns.* terrible, fearful

dusk [dusk] *n.* The time just between sunset and nightfall: **It is hard to see where you are going at *dusk* before the streetlights come on.**

du·ty [d(y)oo′tē] *n.* Something that should be done because it is right or important: **Police officers have a *duty* to keep people safe.**

edge [ej] *n.* **edg·es** The line where a thing begins or ends: **Tomeka put the dishes near the *edges* of the table to make room for the turkey.**

edges

em·brace [im·brās′] *v.* **em·braced** To hug: **Their arms went around each other as they *embraced*.**

ep·i·cen·ter [ep′i·sen′tər] *n.* The place on the earth's surface that is right above the point where an earthquake begins: **Scientists said that the *epicenter* of the earthquake was five miles south of the city.**

e·ven·tu·al·ly [i·ven′choo·əl·ē] *adv.* Over time; in the end: **At first the kitten was afraid, but *eventually* it learned to trust us.** *syn.* finally

fare [fâr] **far·ing** *v.* To get along; to manage: **We were** *faring* **just fine on our nature walk until a skunk crossed our path.**

fare·well [fâr·wel′] *n.* Words spoken when leaving; a good-bye: **As Teresa was leaving, she told her friends** *farewell.*

feast [fēst] *n.* A special meal with a large amount of food: **The king gave a great** *feast* **to celebrate his daughter's wedding.** *syn.* banquet

fluo·res·cent [floŏ·res′ənt] *adj.* Describes something that gives off cool light: **Some** *fluorescent* **light bulbs are in the shape of long, white tubes.**

force [fôrs] *n.* Power or energy to cause something to move or to stop moving: **A sailboat uses the** *force* **of the wind to move across the water.** *syn.* strength

fur·row [fûr′ō] *n.* **fur·rows** A long groove or cut made in the ground by a plow or another tool: **The farmer plowed neat** *furrows* **in the soil and planted seeds in them.**

furrows

gal·lop [gal′əp] *v.* **gal·loped** To ride a horse that is running fast: **Henry was in a hurry to get home, so he got on his horse and** *galloped* **across the field.**

gaze [gāz] *v.* **gaz·ing** To look at something in a way that shows great interest or wonder: **Jamal spent hours** *gazing* **at the clouds as they moved and changed.** *syn.* stare

glis·ten [glis′ən] *v.* **glis·tened** To shine or sparkle: **The lake** *glistened* **in the sunshine.**

growth [grōth] *n.* Plants or things that become greater in size and number in a certain place: **There was a** *growth* **of weeds around the empty house.**

har·vest [här′vist] *v.* To pick or gather a crop, such as grain, fruits, or vegetables: **When the apples are ripe, it's time to** *harvest* **them.**

Word Origins

harvest Until the 1700s, *harvest* named the season we now know as *autumn*. That was the time when many crops were picked.

home·ward [hōm′wərd] *adv.* Toward home: **After we walked to the pond and fed the ducks, we turned** *homeward.*

a	add	e	end	o	odd	o͞o	pool	oi	oil	th	this
ā	ace	ē	equal	ō	open	u	up	ou	pout	zh	vision
â	care	i	it	ô	order	û	burn	ng	ring		
ä	palm	ī	ice	o͝o	took	yo͞o	fuse	th	thin		

ə = {
a in *above*
e in *sicken*
i in *possible*
o in *melon*
u in *circus*
}

land·mark [land′märk′] *n.* An outstanding object in a landscape, such as a building or a mountain: **The oak tree on the corner serves as a *landmark* for finding our street.**

latch [lach] *v.* To close and fasten shut: **Be sure to *latch* the door with a strong lock.**

loop [loop] *v.* **loops** To move in a circle or an oval: **The plane leaves a white trail as it *loops* across the sky.**

loop

ma·chet·e [mə·shet′ē *or* mə·shet′] *n.* A large knife with a heavy blade, often used as a tool, especially in Latin American countries: **Manuel uses a *machete* to cut sugarcane in the fields.**

mag·ma [mag′mə] *n.* Very hot, partly melted rock inside the earth: **Can you imagine how hot it must be inside the earth to melt rocks into *magma*?**

mar·ket [mär′kit] *n.* A place where goods are sold: **After the peaches are picked, trucks take them to the *market* to be sold.**

min·er [mīn′ər] *n.* **min·ers** A person who digs minerals from the earth: **Gold *miners* dig large holes in search of gold.**

mis·chief [mis′chif] *n.* Action that is naughty or that may cause harm: **My mother has to watch my younger brother all the time to keep him out of *mischief*.**

non·sense [non′sens′] *n.* Something that is silly or that does not make sense: **The story about pigs flying is *nonsense*.** *syn.* foolishness

nu·cle·us [n(y)oo′klē·əs] *n.* The center of something: **The pit is the *nucleus* of a peach.**

nug·get [nug′it] *n.* **nug·gets** A lump, especially of gold: **These *nuggets* are valuable pieces.**

out·stretched [out′strecht′] *adj.* Extended out: **His *outstretched* arms reached for the flying ball.**

par·ti·cle [pär′ti·kəl] *n.* **par·ti·cles** A very tiny bit of something: **Did you know that grains of sand are really *particles* of broken rock?**

peak [pēk] *n.* The pointed top of a hill or mountain: **This mountain *peak* is so high that there is always snow on it, even in summer.**

peak

pride [prīd] *n.* A feeling of being proud or having respect for; a feeling of worth: **We keep our streets clean and safe because we have *pride* in our city.**

prof•it [prof′it] *n.* Money gained by selling something: **After Carlos and Isabel paid for the lemons and sugar, they found that they hadn't made much *profit* from selling lemonade.**

pulp [pulp] *n.* The soft, juicy inside of some fruits and vegetables: **Eat the *pulp* of the melon, not the skin.**

ranch•er [ran′chər] *n.* **ranch•ers** A person who owns a large farm for raising animals, such as cattle, sheep, or horses: ***Ranchers* need a lot of land so that their animals will have enough grass to eat.**

range [rānj] *n.* A row or line of mountains: **The mountain *range* looks small on the map, but it is long in real life.**

range

re•ceive [ri•sēv′] *v.* To get something: **I like to give gifts, and I like to *receive* them, too.**

sat•is•fy [sat′is•fī] *v.* **sat•is•fied** To meet someone's needs or wishes: **Dawn kept changing her picture until she was *satisfied* with the way it looked.** *syn.* please

schoon•er [skoo′nər] *n.* A sailing ship that has two or more masts, or poles, that hold up the sails: **We saw a model of an old-fashioned *schooner* at the ship museum.**

schooner

a	add	e	end	o	odd	o͞o	pool	oi	oil	t͟h	this		*a* in *above*
ā	ace	ē	equal	ō	open	u	up	ou	pout	zh	vision		*e* in *sicken*
â	care	i	it	ô	order	û	burn	ng	ring			ə =	*i* in *possible*
ä	palm	ī	ice	o͝o	took	yo͞o	fuse	th	thin				*o* in *melon*
													u in *circus*

set·tle [set'əl] *v.* To make a home: **The families will** *settle* **in the country.**

shun [shun] *v.* **shunned** To stay away from: **The duckling was** *shunned* **by the mother hen and her chicks.** *syn.* avoid

sig·nal [sig'nəl] *v.* To use an action, a symbol, or an object to send a message or to make something known: **We tied balloons to our mailbox to** *signal* **my sister's birthday.**

skil·let [skil'it] *n.* A shallow metal pan with a handle: **Mother likes to fry food in her** *skillet.*

skill·ful [skil'fəl] *adj.* Having the ability to do something very well: **Mr. Green is a** *skillful* **carpenter who knows how to build fine houses.**

so·lar wind [sō'lər wind] *n.* A flow of gases or particles given off by the sun: **The** *solar wind* **is different from the kind of wind we have on Earth.**

> **Fact File**
>
> **solar wind** On Earth, hurricane winds can have speeds of 100 miles per hour. In space, the speed of *solar wind* is about 310 miles per *second!* However, the earth's magnetic forces stop particles in the solar wind from reaching the earth.

sol·dier [sōl'jər] *n.* A person who serves in the army: **My grandfather was a** *soldier* **and was wounded in battle.**

sphere [sfir] *n.* An object that has a shape like a ball: **A baseball is a small** *sphere,* **and a beach ball is a larger one.** *syn.* globe

stage·coach [stāj'kōch'] *n.* A carriage pulled by horses and having a regular route for picking up passengers or packages: **The** *stagecoach* **delivered mail to settlers who lived out West.**

stray [strā] *adj.* Wandering or lost: **We helped the** *stray* **dog find its way home.**

stum·ble [stum'bəl] *v.* **stum·bling** To move along in an unsteady way: **We knew that George was sleepy when we saw him** *stumbling* **out of his bedroom.**

sup·port [sə·pôrt'] *v.* To hold the weight of something or someone: **The old wooden bridge isn't strong enough to** *support* **a car.**

swift·ly [swift'lē] *adv.* In a very fast way: **The jet moved** *swiftly* **across the sky.** *syns.* quickly, rapidly

tend [tend] *v.* **tend·ing** To take care of: **The mother bird was busy** *tending* **her babies.**

ten·der [ten'dər] *adj.* Soft and easily injured: **The** *tender* **fruit was bruised from being touched.**

tid·bit [tid′bit′] *n.* A small, very good bit of food: **Jay selected the tastiest *tidbit* from the tray of snacks.**

track [trak] *n.* **tracks** Footprints or other marks left by a person, an animal, or a thing: **We could see from the *tracks* in the snow that a deer had walked there.**

trad·ing [trā′ding] *adj.* Having to do with exchanging goods: **A *trading* post was a place where hunters exchanged animal skins for things they needed.**

u·ni·verse [yōō′nə•vûrs′] *n.* Everything that is, including the Earth, the sun, planets, stars, and all of space: **Earth is like a tiny dot compared to the size of the *universe*.**

> **Word Origins**
> *Universe* comes from *universus*, the Latin word for "whole" or "entire."

ur·gent [ûr′jənt] *adj.* Needing prompt attention: **Kim's *urgent* letter demanded a quick reply.**

val·ue [val′yōō] *n.* How much something is worth: **Even though a dime is smaller in size than a nickel, the dime has a greater *value*.** *syn.* worth

wail [wāl] *v.* **wail·ing** To cry: **The baby was *wailing* to be fed.**

wea·ry [wir′ē] *adj.* Tired: **After a long day, Joan felt *weary* and went straight to bed.**

wind·mill [wind′mil′] *n.* A machine that uses the power of the wind to grind grain, pump water, or do other work: **As the wind blew, the long blades of the *windmill* turned around and around.**

windmill

wits [wits] *n. (pl.)* The ability to think; good sense: **I needed my *wits* about me to find my way home in the snowstorm.**

a add	e end	o odd	ōō pool	oi oil	th̶ this		*a* in *above*
ā ace	ē equal	ō open	u up	ou pout	zh vision		*e* in *sicken*
â care	i it	ô order	û burn	ng ring		ə =	*i* in *possible*
ä palm	ī ice	ŏŏ took	yōō fuse	th thin			*o* in *melon*
							u in *circus*

Index *of* Titles

Page numbers in color refer to biographical information.

and Authors

Acknowledgments

For permission to reprint copyrighted material, grateful acknowledgment is made to the following sources:

George Ancona: Photographs of money by George Ancona from *If You Made a Million* by David M. Schwartz. Photographs copyright © 1989 by George Ancona.

Atheneum Books for Young Readers, Simon & Schuster Children's Publishing Division: I'm in Charge of Celebrations by Byrd Baylor, illustrated by Peter Parnall. Text copyright © 1986 by Byrd Baylor; illustrations copyright © 1986 by Peter Parnall.

Jeanne Bendick: From *Comets and Meteors: Visitors from Space* by Jeanne Bendick. Text copyright © 1991 by Jeanne Bendick.

Boyds Mills Press, Inc.: Leah's Pony by Elizabeth Friedrich, illustrated by Michael Garland. Text copyright © 1996 by Elizabeth Friedrich; illustrations copyright © 1996 by Michael Garland.

Candlewick Press, Inc., Cambridge, MA, on behalf of Walker Books Ltd., London: "Starry, Starry Night" from *Seeing Stars* by James Muirden. Text © 1998 by James Muirden. From *Rocking and Rolling* by Phillip Steele. Text © 1997 by Phillip Steele; illustrations © 1997 by Walker Books Ltd.

Chronicle Books: Alejandro's Gift by Richard E. Albert, illustrated by Sylvia Long. Text copyright © 1994 by Richard E. Albert; illustrations copyright © 1994 by Sylvia Long.

Dial Books for Young Readers, a division of Penguin Putnam Inc.: Why Mosquitoes Buzz in People's Ears: A West African Tale, retold by Verna Aardema, illustrated by Leo and Diane Dillon. Text copyright © 1975 by Verna Aardema; illustrations copyright © 1975 by Leo and Diane Dillon.

Harcourt, Inc.: The Armadillo from Amarillo by Lynne Cherry. Copyright © 1994 by Lynne Cherry. Stamp designs copyright © by United States Postal Service. Reproduction of images courtesy of Gilbert Palmer, the National Aeronautics and Space Administration, the Austin News Agency, Festive Enterprises, Jack Lewis/Texas Department of Transportation, the Baxter Lane Company, Wyco Colour Productions, Frank Burd, and City Sights. *Worksong* by Gary Paulsen, illustrated by Ruth Wright Paulsen. Text copyright © 1997 by Gary Paulsen; illustrations copyright © 1997 by Ruth Wright Paulsen.

HarperCollins Publishers: If You Made a Million by David M. Schwartz, illustrated by Steven Kellogg. Text copyright © 1989 by David M. Schwartz; illustrations copyright © 1989 by Steven Kellogg.

Holiday House, Inc.: The Ant and the Grasshopper by Amy Lowry Poole. Copyright © 2000 by Amy Lowry Poole.

Kalmbach Publishing Co.: The Crowded House by Eva Jacob from *PLAYS: The Drama Magazine for Young People.* Text copyright © 1959, 1970 by Plays, Inc. This play is for reading purposes only; for permission to produce, write to Kalmbach Publishing Co., 21027 Crossroads Circle, P.O. Box 1612, Waukesha, WI 53187-1612.

Kingfisher Publications plc: From "Mapping the World" in *Young Discoverers: Maps and Mapping* by Barbara Taylor, cover illustration by Kevin Maddison. Text and cover illustration copyright © 1992 by Grisewood and Dempsey Ltd.

Little, Brown and Company (Inc.): Yippee-Yay! A Book About Cowboys and Cowgirls by Gail Gibbons. Copyright © 1998 by Gail Gibbons.

Ludlow Music, Inc., New York, NY: "This Land Is Your Land," words and music by Woody Guthrie. TRO—©—copyright 1956 (Renewed) 1958 (Renewed) and 1970 (Renewed) by Ludlow Music, Inc.

Philomel Books, an imprint of Penguin Putnam Books for Young Readers, a division of Penguin Putnam Inc.: Lon Po Po: A Red Riding Hood Story from China, translated and illustrated by Ed Young. Copyright © 1989 by Ed Young.

Scholastic Inc.: Cocoa Ice by Diana Appelbaum, illustrated by Holly Meade. Text copyright © 1997 by Diana Appelbaum; illustrations copyright © 1997 by Holly Meade. Published by Orchard Books, an imprint of Scholastic Inc. *Boom Town* by Sonia Levitin, illustrated by Cat Bowman Smith. Text copyright © 1998 by Sonia Levitin; illustrations copyright © 1998 by Cat Bowman Smith. Published by Orchard Books, an imprint of Scholastic Inc.

Simon & Schuster Books for Young Readers, Simon & Schuster Children's Publishing Division: Papa Tells Chita a Story by Elizabeth Fitzgerald Howard, illustrated by Floyd Cooper. Text copyright © 1994 by Elizabeth Fitzgerald Howard; illustrations copyright © 1994 by Floyd Cooper. *Coyote Places the Stars* by Harriet Peck Taylor. Copyright © 1993 by Harriet Peck Taylor.

Photo Credits

Key: (t)=top; (b)=bottom; (c)=center; (l)=left; (r)=right.
Page 51, Black Star; 52, The Granger Collection, New York; 53(t), Harcourt Photo Library; 53(b), Zefa / H. Armstrong Roberts; 60, Lawrence Migdale / Photo Researchers, Inc.; 113, Tom Sobolik / Black Star; 162, Rick Friedman / Black Star; 163, Black Star; 168, Barry Levy / Index Stock Photography; 169, Superstock; 187, courtesy, Gail Gibbons; 188, National Gallery of Art, Washington, DC; 215(t), Rose Eichenbaum; 215(b), courtesy, Scholastic; 216(t), Nik Wheeler / Corbis; 216(c), C.J. Collins / Photo Researchers, Inc.; 217(t), Walter Coker / Silver Image; 217(b), George E. Jones III / Photo Researchers, Inc.; 222, Superstock; 223(t), Tim Page / Corbis; 223(c), (cb), Harcourt Photo Library; 223(b), Jeff Schultz / AlaskaStock; 254, 255, Rick Friedman / Black Star; 290, Dale Higgins; 291, Tom Sobolik / Black Star; 292, 293, Ken Kinzie / Harcourt; 318, Black Star; 319, Rick Friedman / Black Star; 324, Simon Jauncey / Stone; 325, Mickey Gibson / Earth Scenes; 342, Patti Murray / Earth Scenes; 343, Harry Rogers / Photo Researchers, Inc.; 365, courtesy, Philip Steele; 392, Black Star; 394-395, Corbis Stock Market; 395(t), The Granger Collection, New York; 395(cl), (cr), Harcourt Photo Library; 400, 402(l), 402-403, Aaron Horowitz / Corbis; 410, Corbis; 412, Black Star; 415, Bettmann / Corbis; 445(t), Jim Steinberg / Photo Researchers, Inc.; 445(b), Harcourt Photo Library; 446(l), Gail Shumway / FPG; 446(r), Harcourt Photo Library; 447, Inga Spence / Tom Stack & Associates; 449(tl), Richard Johnston / Stone; 449(br), Joyce Photographics / Photo Researchers, Inc.; 451, Bob Krist / Corbis Stock Market.

Illustration Credits

Dan Craig, Cover Art; Jennie Oppenheimer, 4-5, 12-13; Paul Cox, 6-7, 144-145; Dave LeFleur, 8-9, 298-299; Ethan Long 10-11, 33, 165, 259, 345, 416; Art Valero, 14-15; Floyd Cooper, 16-31; Nancy Davis, 34, 92, 116, 141, 260, 370-371; Lizi Boyd, 36-37; Harriet Peck Taylor, 38-51; Terry Widener, 52-55; Tom Leonard, 55; Cathy Bennett, 57, 58, 191, 321, 367; Leo and Diane Dillon, 62-85; Tracy Sabin, 94-95; Ed Young, 96-113; Jackie Snider, 115; Paul Meisel, 118-119; Holly Cooper, 120-135; Diane Paterson, 136-139; Tuko Fujisaki, 142, 219, 448; Lisa Carlson, 146-147; Michael Garland, 148-163; Chris Van Dusen, 166, 415; Gail Gibbons, 170-187; Thomas Hart Benton, 188; Stephen Snider, 194-195; Laura Ovresat, 220-221; Holly Meade, 224-255; Ruth Wright Paulsen, 256-257; Tracy McGuinness, 262-263; Steven Kellogg, 264-291; Nancy Coffelt, 295, 296, 346, 397; Hideko Takahashi, 300-301; Peter Parnall, 302-319; Sylvia Long, 326-341; Sharron O'Neil, 342-343; Rick Allen, 348-349; Philip Steele, 350-365; Lynne Cherry, 372-393; Richard Hull, 400-401; David Schleinkofer, 402-413.